OSPREY AIRCRAFT OF THE ACES® • 44

Gloster
Gladiator Aces

SERIES EDITOR: TONY HOLMES

OSPREY AIRCRAFT OF THE ACES® • 44

Gloster Gladiator Aces

Andrew Thomas

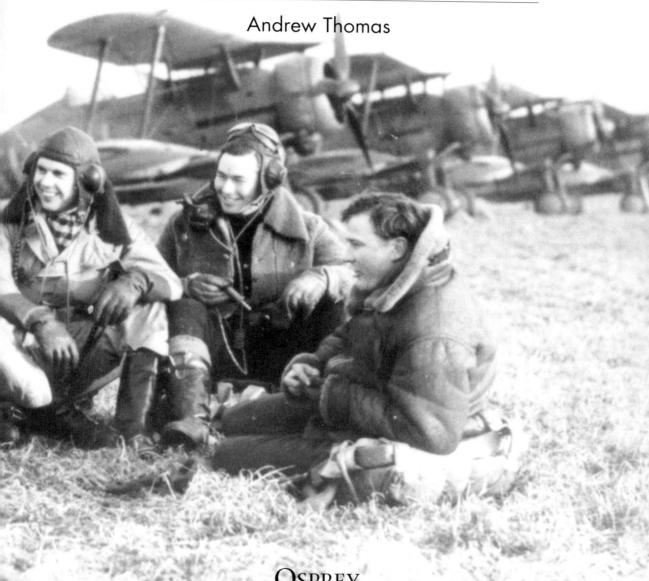

OSPREY
PUBLISHING

Front cover
Late in the afternoon of 4 August 1940, four Gladiators of 'B' Flight No 80 Sqn were ordered to escort a Lysander of No 208 Sqn that was to fly a reconnaissance mission over Italian positions in the Bir Taieb el Esem area, some 30 miles inside the Libyan border. The patrol was led by Flt Lt 'Pat' Pattle in Gladiator I K7910, with Flg Off Johnny Lancaster (in K7923) as his 'number two', whilst the second section was led by Flg Off Peter Wykeham-Barnes in L8009/YK-I, with Sgt Kenneth Rew (flying K7908) as his wingman. At 1815 hrs, as they neared their target, the Lysander was threatened by a formation of enemy aircraft and it dived away. The No 208 Sqn machine had encountered seven Breda Ba.65 attack bombers of the El Adem-based 159° *Squadriglia*, 12° *Gruppo Assalto* of 50° *Stormo*, led by Capitano Antonio Dell 'Oro. They were flying in two formations – one of four aircraft and one of three. The Ba.65s had been attacking British positions, and were accompanied by Fiat CR.32s of 160° *Squadriglia*, led by Capitano Duilio Fanali.

Wykeham-Barnes called 'Tally Ho!' and dived on the flight of four Bredas, which was threatening the Lysander. He engaged the left-hand aircraft and it quickly caught fire and went down, thus becoming No 80 Sqn's first Gladiator kill. Kenneth Rew attacked the right-hand Breda as it broke formation, but he was himself attacked by the Fiat fighters and shot down and killed by Fanali. Wykeham-Barnes also became embroiled with the fighters, being credited with downing one, but he too was severely hit by the CR.32 flown by Maresciallo Romolo Cantelli, and obliged to bail out. He was picked up by a patrol from the 11th Hussars the following morning.

Pattle and Lancaster also joined the fight, falling on the second formation of three Bredas. Pattle downed one of them to claim the first of his estimated 50+ victories. Lancaster was hit by Cantelli and wounded in the left arm and shoulder, but he managed to crash-land at Sidi Barrani – his aircraft was written off. Pattle, too, was engaged by the CR.32s and shot one down before escaping to the east. However, south of El Adem, he was attacked by 12 Fiat CR.42s, and with his one remaining gun jammed, Pattle eventually succumbed to their fire and bailed out at 1915 hrs. He too was picked up by the 11th Hussars during the course of the following afternoon.

This specially commissioned cover painting by Ian Wyllie shows Peter Wykeham-Barnes, having attacked and set one of the Ba.65s on fire, about to turn and face the imminent threat of Romolo Cantelli's Fiat CR.32

First published in Great Britain in 2002 by Osprey Publishing, Elms Court, Chapel Way, Botley, Oxford, OX2 9LP

ISBN 1 84176 289 X

Edited by Tony Holmes
Page design by Tony Truscott
Cover Artwork by Iain Wyllie
Aircraft Profiles by John Weal
Scale Drawings by Mark Styling
Origination by Grasmere Digital Imaging, Leeds, UK
Printed through Bookbuilders, Hong Kong

02 03 04 05 06   10 9 8 7 6 5 4 3 2 1

Editor's note
To make this best-selling series as authoritative as possible, the Editor would be interested in hearing from any individual who may have relevant photographs, documentation or first-hand experiences relating to the world's elite pilots and units, and the aircraft they flew, in the various theatres of war. Any material used will be credited to its original source. Please write to Tony Holmes at 10 Prospect Road, Sevenoaks, Kent, TN13 3UA, Great Britain, or by e-mail at: tony.holmes@osprey-jets.freeserve.co.uk

Acknowledgements
The author wishes to record his gratitude to the following former Gladiator pilots who have given of their time in patiently answering questions and presenting accounts of their actions for inclusion within this volume – Sqn Ldr J M V Carpenter DFC & Bar, Wg Cdr E H Dean, Air Marshal Sir Patrick Dunn KBE, CB, DFC, the late Gp Capt R S Mills DFC, Sqn Ldr P F Morfill DFM, the late Wg Cdr J R Kayll DSO, OBE, DFC, Wg Cdr H H Kitchener DFM, Wg Cdr P L Parrott DFC & Bar, AFC, Wg Cdr T Rowland, Wg Cdr J G Sanders DFC, the late Gp Capt D F B Sheen DFC & Bar and Cdr J W Sleigh DSO, OBE, DSC.

The author is also most grateful to the many friends and fellow enthusiasts, too numerous to mention, who have generously given of their time and material to bring this volume to fruition.

CONTENTS

COMBAT DEBUT

That the Gladiator entered service as the RAF's last biplane fighter is a monument to conservative thinking in the mid-1930s, though fortunately RAF Fighter Command had largely re-equipped with the eight-gun monoplane Hurricane and Spitfire by the start of the war. The Gladiator was, however, an important type during the expansion of the RAF during the late 1930s, with many of the successful pilots in the air battles of the early years of World War 2 cutting their teeth with it during the final halcyon years of peace. Gladiator units remained in the frontline into 1941, their pilots flying in often desperate circumstances against the odds. In the process, they wrote some of the most gallant episodes in the annals of the RAF.

That these men, and their counterparts in several foreign air forces, achieved the success they did is testament not only to their courage, but also the inherent flying qualities of the Gladiator. Some pilots made large scores flying the type – indeed 'Pat' Pattle, now recognised as the Commonwealth's top scoring fighter pilot, claimed around a third of his victories on the Gladiator.

PRE-WAR SERVICE

The Gladiator entered RAF service with the newly formed No 72 Sqn at Tangmere on 22 February 1937. In temporary command was Flt Lt Teddy Donaldson (later Air Commodore CB, CBE, DSO, AFC), who became an ace flying Hurricanes with No 151 Sqn in 1940. Having taken delivery of its aircraft (K6130-K6144), No 72 got to grips with its new mounts at its new permanent base at Church Fenton. The squadron was typical of the time, with experienced flight commanders, but with most of the pilots coming straight from flying training. No 72 contained in the ranks of its young pilots those who were soon to make their mark.

One of the latter was Australian Plt Off Des Sheen, who, with remarkable memory, recalled those days to the author:

'Our aircraft on delivery were aluminium overall, but after the squadron crest was approved, the "Swift" was added to the fins. OC "A" Flight, Flt Lt F M Smith (who later made around five air combat claims in 1940-41 – author) usually flew K6130. Other notable pilots of "A" Flight, with "their" aircraft, were K6131 – Flg Off J C Boulter (4 or 5 victories – author), K6132 – Flg Off J B Nicholson (later awarded the Victoria Cross during the Battle of Britain – author) and K6133 – Flg Off J W "Pancho" Villa (13 and 4 shared destroyed – author). The "B" Flight pilots' aircraft included K6142 – Flg Off J B Humpherson (five victories – author), K6143 –

During the late 1930s the RAF placed much emphasis on formation flying skills, as typified here by this trio from No 72 Sqn in 1938. Flg Off Henswick leads two future aces, Flg Offs J B Humpherson in K6142 and Des Sheen in K6143 (*D F B Sheen*)

myself (4 and 1 shared victories – author) and finally K6144 – Flg Off "Jimmy" Elsdon (seven victories – author).'

No 72 Sqn retained its Gladiators through the Munich Crisis of September 1938, when it was placed onto a war footing, but replacement Spitfire Is arrived in April 1939. This was not the last that the unit saw of the biplane, however. Des Sheen remembers:

'Early in the war (from 2 March 1940 – author) we were operating out of the sodden grass airfield at Acklington, mainly on convoy patrols. You dare not try to move a Spitfire without one or preferably two sitting on the tailplane. The CO, Ronnie Lees, got a couple of Gladiators for pre-dawn take-offs in particular. Taking off on a Glim Light Flare Path with spray and mud flying past the cockpit was quite an experience, but no problem for the Gladiator. It was a lovely aircraft to fly, and I was fortunate to be a pilot of it.'

After No 72, further units re-equipped, with the next being Kenley-based No 3 at the beginning of April. Future aces flying Gladiators with this squadron included Plt Off C A C 'Bunny' Stone (5 and 2 shared destroyed) and Sgt R C 'Wilkie' Wilkinson, who claimed 7 and 2 shared during the Battle of France. Another new squadron was No 80, soon to become the leading exponents of the Gladiator. The first examples for No 54 Sqn, at Hornchurch, arrived on 27 April 1937, and amongst its pilots were the likes of Plt Off Johnny Allen (7½ confirmed destroyed), Flg Off 'Prof' Leathart (7½ destroyed) and the legendary New Zealander Plt Off Al Deere (17½ destroyed, 4 probables and 7½ damaged).

Sharing Hornchurch with No 54 was another distinguished squadron, No 65, which collected its aircraft straight from the Gloster factory on 14 May 1937. This unit also included several future 'aces', one of whom was the then Plt Off Bob Stanford Tuck – he would claim 27 and 2 shared victories before being shot down and made a PoW. Others included Plt Off Brian Kingcome (8 and 3 shared destroyed) and sergeant pilot Percy Morfill, who was decorated with the DFM and claimed 6½ enemy aircraft destroyed during the Battles of France and Britain. When asked about the introduction of the Gladiator to No 65 Sqn, he recalled:

'I was in No 65 Sqn from early 1937 until 1940, and will always remember collecting our new Gladiators. Our CO was one of the old school, and he came back to Hornchurch with the hood open all the way, and landed without using the flaps! He disliked these new

All of these pilots from No 72 Sqn, photographed in 1938, would see action within the next two years, and some were to meet with considerable success. Many did not survive the war, however. They are, from left to right, Flt Lt F M Smith (2½ destroyed/1 probable/1 damaged, wounded in action) and Flg Offs J B Nicholson (later to win Fighter Command's only VC, killed in action), J B Humpherson (5/2/3, killed in action), D F B Sheen (6½/2/2, wounded in action), O StJ Pigg (killed in action), R A Thompson (wounded in action) and T A F Elsdon (7/1/2, wounded in action) (*D F B Sheen*)

Flg Off J B Nicholson pulls his aircraft in tight for a photograph in February 1939. After the Munich Crisis, the Gladiators were camouflaged and unit code letters added – 'RN' in No 72's case. On 16 August 1940, Nicholson won Fighter Command's sole VC whilst serving with No 249 Sqn (*R L Ward*)

ideas, especially the flaps, which he said upset the trim! No 65 Sqn formed a flight formation team in early 1938, which was led by Flt Lt Bicknell, with Flg Off Tuck (usually in K8015 – author) as 'number two' and myself as number three on the left (usually flying K8013 – author). We had to do many shows, including the old Empire Air Day, and all went well until Tuck collided with the leader, causing him to bail out.

Hornchurch-based No 65 Sqn flew Gladiators for almost two years, and included within its ranks several future aces. Amongst them was Sgt Percy Morfill, who flew K8013 with 'B' Flight. He was part of the aerobatic team with fellow future ace Plt Off R R S Tuck (*P F Morfill*)

'Yes, the Gladiator was a very nice aeroplane to fly, but we did, however, look forward to getting our Spitfire Is in early 1939.'

Four more regular squadrons in Fighter Command – Nos 56, 73, 85 and 87 – received the Gladiator, although all had re-equipped with Hurricane Is by late 1938. One particularly noteworthy pilot flying with No 73 Sqn during its brief period with the Gloster fighter was Plt Off E J 'Cobber' Kain, who later became the RAF's first 'ace' of World War 2, before losing his life in a flying accident on 5 June 1940. With another future ace, Flg Off 'Fanny' Orton, he gave exhibitions of aerobatics at the 1938 Empire Air Day.

From late 1938, surplus Gladiators were passed to squadrons of the Auxiliary Air Force, starting with No 607 'County of Durham' Sqn, which became the only auxiliary unit to claim a kill with the type. No 605 'County of Warwick' Sqn followed suit in February 1939, as did Nos 603 'City of Edinburgh' and 615 'County of Surrey' Sqns. Each of these units contained a number of future aces, and they would all play a key role in the defence of Britain during 1940.

A fully navalised version, christened the Sea Gladiator, entered Royal Navy service with 801 Naval Air Squadron (NAS) on 28 February 1939. 801 NAS was shore-based at Donibristle, but the unit spent embarked periods on the aircraft carrier HMS *Courageous*, where it was mainly employed conducting deck landing training (DLT). Amongst its pilots was Lt J M 'Bill' Bruen, who, whilst serving in the Mediterranean in

Sea Gladiator N5500 was assigned to the Fleet Air Arm's 769 NAS, which formed at Donibristle, in Fife, in mid-1939 to undertake deck landing training for naval pilots. This machine was frequently flown by instructor Lt 'Bill' Bruen, who later became an ace with 803 NAS in 1940-41 (*J M Bruen*)

1940-41, was credited with eight kills. At the end of May 1939 801 NAS was renumbered as 769 NAS, with Bruen as one of its instructors. 802 NAS, embarked in HMS *Glorious*, was later re-equipped as the only operational Sea Gladiator unit.

INTO ACTIVE SERVICE

In March 1938 No 33 Sqn at Ismailia, in Egypt, replaced its Harts with Gladiators, retraining in the fighter role for the defence of the Suez Canal. It was joined in May by No 80 Sqn, which had been posted overseas. Both squadrons were blessed with a plethora of talent, No 33 including in its ranks Sgt Bill 'Cherry' Vale who, with 10 and 2 shared kills, would come second only to Pattle in claims with the Gladiator. In mid-1939, Canadian Plt Off Vernon 'Woody' Woodward joined the unit, and his final score of 18 and 4 shared victories included 4 and 2 shared on Gladiators. Amongst No 80's pilots was South African Flg Off M T StJ Pattle, known universally as 'Pat'. Another was Plt Off Ernest 'Dixie' Dean, who held Pattle in the highest regard:

'Pattle was actually the adjutant of 80. A quiet, pleasant South African, he was a superb pilot. After moving to our war station ten miles from Alexandria, we started in earnest with air-to-ground and air-to-air gunnery. Here, "Pat" showed his superiority in deflection shooting in gaining many more hits than any of the other pilots in the unit.'

Both squadrons saw active service in Palestine assisting the British garrison in containing a virtual civil war between Arabs and Jews, the units sending detachments to Ramleh through the summer of 1938, from where

Seen at Ramleh, in Palestine, during policing operations conducted by No 33 Sqn, Gladiator I K8036 carries the squadron's code letters SO on its otherwise peacetime finish. It was regularly flown by Sgt Bill Vale, who was to fly the type with distinction over the desert and Greece in 1940-41 (*No 33 Sqn Records*)

With the Ismailia airship mast providing a distinctive backdrop, two Gladiators Is of No 80 Sqn prepare for take-off in the spring of 1939. The nearest one (K7903/OD-B), assigned to Flt Lt E G Jones, wears unit codes and also the squadron's badge on its red-coloured fin. It was shot down by Italian CR.42s on 8 August 1940 (*E G Jones*)

On 28 July 1938, soon after No 80 Sqn had arrived in Egypt, Plt Off Pattle was air-testing Gladiator I K8009 when the engine cut and the aircraft briefly struck the ground, tearing off its port wheel. Showing his skills as a pilot, Pattle landed the aircraft at Ismailia without inflicting further damage, and it was flying again later that day! This aircraft later took part in No 80 Sqn's first Gladiator combat on 4 August 1940 (*A T Phillips*)

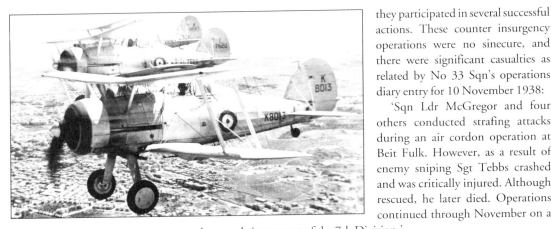

Sqn Ldr H D McGregor (in K8013) leads a section of Gladiators from No 33 Sqn over Jerusalem during policing operations in late 1938. His machine does not yet carry any unit codes, although it wears the CO's rank pennant beneath the cockpit (*author's collection*)

In the spring of 1939 No 33 Sqn's unit codes changed to TN, and its Gladiators were given a local, and very rough, camouflage scheme, as evidenced by L7619 at Ismailia. This fighter was regularly flown by future Canadian ace Plt Off Vernon Woodward (*author's collection*)

they participated in several successful actions. These counter insurgency operations were no sinecure, and there were significant casualties as related by No 33 Sqn's operations diary entry for 10 November 1938:

'Sqn Ldr McGregor and four others conducted strafing attacks during an air cordon operation at Beit Fulk. However, as a result of enemy sniping Sgt Tebbs crashed and was critically injured. Although rescued, he later died. Operations continued through November on a large scale in support of the 7th Division.'

Operations in this period of air policing had been intense, and between September and December No 33 flew 1,850 hours, losing two pilots killed and two injured, as well as three aircraft destroyed. After the squadron returned to Egypt a number of pilots were decorated, including a DSO for the New Zealander, McGregor, who as CO of No 213 Sqn during the Battle of Britain, claimed around six aircraft shot down. He later became Air Marshal Sir Hector McGregor, KCB, DSO, CBE.

By the outbreak of war, the only Fighter Command units with Gladiators were the four auxiliary squadrons. Overseas in Egypt, Nos 33 and 80 Sqns had been joined by a newly formed No 112 Sqn, whilst in Aden No 94 had been formed to defend the port and Red Sea approaches.

CHINA – THE COMBAT DEBUT

It is a little known fact that the Gladiator's combat career actually began in 1938 in the skies of eastern China. In October 1937, during the height of the Sino-Japanese War, an order for 36 Gladiator Is was placed with Glosters by the Chinese Central Government. The aircraft were desperately needed by the Chinese, who contracted for early delivery, and the first 20 arrived by sea in Hong Kong in late November. They were to be erected at the RAF base at Kai Tak, but due to Japanese diplomatic pressure, the crated aircraft were moved firstly by rail and then river junk to Guangzhou. Assembly in the face of enemy air attacks proved problematical, but by January 1938 they had been erected at a number of sites ranging from Tienhe air base to a cemetery!

After testing, the completed aircraft were moved inland out of range of marauding Japanese aircraft for a spell of pilot training, during which time the inexperienced Chinese pilots wrote off several machines. This first batch, serialled 5701-5720 (but usually identified by the unit's number and two-digit aircraft code, such as '2909'), were then issued to the Gunzhou-based 28th and 29th Pursuit Squadrons (PS) of the 5th Pursuit Group (PG). The second batch of 16 aircraft – 5721-5736 – were delivered in January 1938, and these were duly issued to the two units. Later, the 3rd PG's 32nd PS also received a handful of Gladiators. By early February 1938, the fighters were ready for operations, and the biplanes proved a useful addition to the Chinese Air Force, which operated a mix of Soviet, US and Italian fighters.

The Gladiator's combat debut came over eastern China in 1938, following the delivery of 36 fighters to the Central Government. They were assembled under difficult conditions in various locations, this poor but rare photograph showing one being wheeled out for testing after assembly (*author's collection*)

The Gladiator's combat debut came early on the morning of 24 February 1938 when a formation of Imperial Japanese Navy E8N 'Dave' floatplanes, escorted by A5M 'Claude' fighters flew a reconnaissance mission over the Nanking area. Three Gladiators from the 28th and nine from the 29th PS, led by the latter unit's commander, Chinese-American Capt John Wong Sun-Shui (nicknamed 'Buffalo'), scrambled from Nan Hsuang and split into two sections.

Wong, who already had two kills to his name, led one section, but it was the other which first spotted the enemy at 6,000 ft in their 'nine o'clock'. Diving on the unsuspecting Japanese, several of the Chinese pilots quickly damaged two of the A5Ms. Signalling his section to follow, 'Buffalo' Wong led his men into the fight, and the 'Claude' which fell to his fire became the Gladiator's first victim. Wong is then believed to have shot down a second A5M, for the remains of two Japanese fighters were duly found. The Gladiator's debut in action was not, however, a one-sided affair, for two were shot down and others damaged by the nimble Navy fighters. The fight also highlighted a high rate of gun malfunctions.

There were several further scrambles on succeeding days, culminating in a further success for 'Buffalo' Wong on the 28th (also quoted as the 25th). Having taken off from Tienhe at 2005 hrs on a lone patrol, he intercepted four E8Ns along the Kowloon – Guangzhou railway, and records state that he destroyed a single floatplane – his third kill with the Gladiator and fifth overall.

Following a brief lull in the fighting, the next major engagement for the Chinese Gladiators came on 13 April. That morning, eight D1A 'Susie' dive-bombers (led by Lt Nishihara) from the carrier *Kaga*, with an escort of nine A4N biplanes and eight A5M 'Claudes', raided the Canton area.

'Buffalo' Wong led off nine Gladiators of the 29th PS for base defence from Teinhe at 1020 hrs, whilst an identical number from the 28th, led by fellow Chinese-American Capt Clifford ('Long Legged') Louie Yim-Qun, set off to intercept the raiders. The enemy was sighted north-west of the base at 13,000 ft, with the escorts flying in five 'Vee' formations. As the Gladiators reached 16,000 ft, Wong (flying 2913) waggled his wings and led his men down into the bombers. In one pass, he shot a D1A down in flames before the escort arrived.

In the stiff turning fight that ensued, Wong also despatched an A4N into the banks of the Pearl River, before wading single-handed into the A5Ms. As tracer flew past him, he pulled hard right and the A5M on his tail overshot him. Despite having only one gun working, he was nonetheless able to down a 'Claude' before being overwhelmed – Plt Off 1/c Chono, having overshot the Gladiator, turned back into the Chinese fighter and this time hit the Gladiator hard with a series of bursts. Wong was forced to bail out, having been struck in the arm.

Whilst hanging beneath his 'chute, he saw his wingman, Li Yu-rong, destroy another A5M before being downed near Sun Yat Sen University.

Others within the squadron also made claims, including Lt Teng Chung-kai, who intervened when Li and Lt Huang Kwang-ching were bounced. Going for Huang's attackers, he disrupted them long enough to allow his colleagues to escape – he also downed one of the A4Ns in flames. Teng then went after another biplane fighter, which he also claimed shot down – he later flew I-15s, and ended with a total of 2 and 2 shared destroyed and 2 damaged.

Leading his formation into the action, Clifford Louie claimed one of the dive-bombers destroyed – it dived away streaming smoke. He attacked and hit another, flown by Plt Off 1/c Tanaka, which limped off spewing oil and smoke before being ditched in the mouth of the Pearl River. With his guns now jammed, Louie climbed out of the fight and watched further Japanese aircraft fall away. The Gladiators continued to patrol at high altitude before landing. The battle had lasted 40 minutes, after which the Chinese pilots claimed nine destroyed for the loss of four, with several other Gladiators damaged to varying degrees. The Japanese admitted the loss of at least five aircraft.

FIRST GLADIATOR ACE

Action for the gradually decreasing number of Gladiators next came on the last day of May. At 1300 hrs, nine Japanese aircraft were detected nearing Hukou, and 'Buffalo' Wong led off four pilots which soon sighted nine E8Ns in 'vee' formation at 6,000 ft – some 1,500 ft below them. He rolled in and dived to attack the Japanese, who manoeuvred wildly to escape. Following a lengthy fight, Wong eventually brought one down near Chenjaixin, killing the crew. Another fell to his wingman, and the remaining pilots damaged several more before the Gladiators withdrew unscathed.

This kill gave 'Buffalo' Wong his seventh, and final, victory, and it was his fifth claim with the Gladiator, making him the first ace on type. He was later promoted to command the 5th FLG, but was shot down in a combat with A6M Zeros on 14 March 1941 and died two days later.

The commander of the 5th PG in mid-1938 was yet another Chinese-American, Maj John Wong Pan-Yang, who had already claimed five Japanese aircraft destroyed flying the Boeing 281 (P-26 'Peashooter').

The intensity of Japanese air attacks had been increasing through the summer of 1938, and on the morning of 16 June the Takao Kokutai of the JNAF mounted two attacks in the Nanking area. Six G3M 'Nell' twin-engined bombers in two 'vics', led by Lt Yoneda and Lt(jg) Iwaya, approached as Wong Pan-Yang (flying 2909) led off eight Gladiators from Xiaoquan. Lt Teng Chung-kai in 2809 spotted the intruders 2,000 ft below them and led the fighters into the second vic.

Wong attacked Yoneda's aircraft, employing his favourite tactic – approaching the bomber from below, in its defensive blind-spot. He hit the

Maj John Wong Pan-Yang of the 5th FG claimed four kills with Gladiator 2909 on 16 June 1938 whilst defending Nanking (*author's collection*)

The only known identifiable photograph of a Chinese Gladiator shows 2909 of the 29th PS, and was probably taken at Tienhe in early 1938. It participated in several combats, and was flown by the 5th PG CO, Maj John Wong Pan-Yang, on 16 June 1938 when he destroyed a G3M 'Nell' bomber and shared in the destruction of three others (*author's collection*)

'Nells' external bomb-load, which detonated in dramatic fashion, turning the bomber into a fireball. It crashed near the target. Capt Arthur Chin Shui-tin, flying 2808, attacked the bomber to the left of the vic, and it too went down in flames – he then attacked a third. Wong, meanwhile, had suffered the frustration of having his guns jam.

Pilots flying other types also joined the fray, and during this epic combat in which two Gladiators were lost, five of the bombers were claimed, although only three were in fact destroyed. Wong, whose aircraft was damaged by the exploding 'Nell', was credited with one and three shared victories. These were his only claims with the Gladiator in his eventual total of four and five shared.

Pilots flying the Gloster fighter were finding it increasingly difficult to hold their own against the modern A5M, and because of a lack of spares due to an arms embargo, the surviving Gladiators would eventually be relegated to the training role. However, before they could be replaced, they were to take part in one of the biggest battles yet seen in China's skies.

In the early morning of 3 August, 18 G3Ms were detected heading for Hankow, followed some time later by an estimated 70 fighters. The Chinese managed to scramble over 50 fighters, in four groups, to defend the city. The fourth of these groups included 11 Gladiators in A and B sub-groups, the latter being led by 'Art' Chin in 2806.

Leadership of sub-group A also devolved on one of the Gladiator pilots, namely Capt Chu Chia-hsun of the 32nd PS. Engaging the enemy, Chu lead his group in to attack a gaggle of A5Ms that had surrounded an I-15. His fire punctured the wing of a 'Claude', and his wingman, He Jermin, downed another A5M – the wreckage fell into Lake Chaoping.

Chin's sub-group, meanwhile, had climbed to 12,000 ft south-west of the city, before climbing further still into a group of 30 A5Ms. Louis Yim-Qun was duly attacked, and although his Gladiator was badly damaged, he shot his attacker down with the help of another pilot, possibly Chin. Going to the aid of yet another of his men (Lt Fan Hsin-min), Chin damaged another 'Claude', but he soon found himself fighting for his life as three A5Ms took it in turns to attack him. His aircraft was badly hit, with rigging wires shot away and other damage making it almost uncontrollable. However, as one of his tormentors climbed after a firing pass, 'Art' Chin reversed his turn and rammed the enemy fighter, ripping its wing off. The Chinese pilot then managed to bail out, with some difficulty.

GUERRILLA CAMPAIGN

These latest losses left just nine Gladiators available, and later in the month they were transferred to the charge of the 32nd PS. Just before 1000 hrs on 30 August, enemy bombers were again reported heading for Hankow. In a last ditch effort to defend the city, the Chinese scrambled all nine, led by the 3rd PG's CO, Lt Col Wu Yu-Liu. He led one section of five, whilst Capt Chu Chia-hsun, commander of the 32nd FS, led the remainder. By the time they were airborne, at 1030 hrs, the D1A dive-bombers had completed their mission and were heading home.

However, further Japanese formations were then reported heading for Nanking, to where Wu led his fighters. They missed a second group of 18 D1As, but at 1040 hrs the Gladiators engaged a third formation from the carrier *Kaga*, comprising 11 D1As and an equal number of A5Ms. A battle lasting some 45 minutes ensued, Chu attacking the 'Claudes' and sending two of them down – this made him the only ace of the former Kwangsi Provisional Air Force. The JNAF admitted the losses of Lt Teshima (*Kaga's* Divisional Officer) and PO2/c Sugino.

The 32nd PS's biplanes had suffered heavily, however, with Lt Col Wu being killed and another pilot later dying of wounds. A third crash-landed and was injured and three others bailed out. It was the end for the Chinese Gladiators – almost. The remaining aircraft were sent to Liu-Chow, in Kwangsi, for overhaul, and the following August (1939) Maj 'Art' Chin, now deputy commander of the 3rd FLG, and two others ferried the three Gladiators to Lanchow, from where they conducted a 'guerrilla' campaign during the Japanese invasion of Kwangsi.

On 2 November 1939 he damaged a Ki-15 'Babs' reconnaissance aircraft, although his wingman failed to finish it off. Chin's next claim came just before Christmas, when he recorded destroying a 'twin-engined' bomber over Kwangsi. He recalled 'downing it by diving and then pulling up to hit its belly'. Chin's final combat came on the 27th, when his two Gladiators and an I-15 provided escort for Soviet-manned SB-2 bombers during the Battle for the Kunlan Pass.

When flying over Yunping, the three fighters became engaged with a group of A5Ms, probably from the 14th Kokutai. The I-15 was forced down, and Chin apparently shot down an A5M, although the other Gladiator fell despite Chin shooting a 'Claude' off its tail. He was then hit from behind, and his fuel tank exploded. Chin bailed out with terrible burns, and he was fired on during his descent. He recalled:

'They tried to shoot me all the way down to the jungle. I hurt a lot, but I slumped in the parachute pretending to be dead. I could hear the bullets whizzing past me.'

Chin was taken to hospital in Hong Kong, from where he escaped following the Japanese occupation. All but two of his 8½ kills had been scored in the Gladiator, making him the leading Chinese ace on the type.

The most successful Chinese Gladiator pilot was Capt 'Art' Chin Shui-tin of the 28th FS who in 1938–39 claimed 6½ victories on the British biplane out of his 8½ total. He was badly burned during his final Gladiator combat and after treatment in Hong Kong, eventually escaped to the USA *(R Cheung)*

THE PHONEY WAR

From the outbreak of World War 2, reconnaissance flights by the Luft-waffe of British naval bases had led to occasional clashes. Fighter patrols were instigated as a result of these flights, and one of the first by a Gladiator was flown on 5 September by Flt Lt George Denholm of No 603 Sqn – it proved to be uneventful. Almost immediately, the unit began training on Spitfires. On 10 October No 607 Sqn moved to Acklington to serve alongside newly formed No 152, and it was from here that the auxiliary squadron went into action one week later. The only surviving pilot of No 607's action is William H R Whitty, who recalled for the author:

'Mid-morning on 17 October, my section (Flt Lt J Sample, Flg Off G D Craig and Plt Off W H R Whitty of "B" Flight – author) was sent off

Seen during the last halcyon days of peace in 1939, these camouflaged Gladiators of No 607 Sqn are parked at Abbotsinch between sorties during the unit's summer camp. They were soon in action, for No 607 Sqn claimed the RAF's first Gladiator victory on 17 October 1939 (*No 607 Sqn Records*)

Leading the No 607 Sqn section that downed a Do 18 on 16 October 1939 was Flt Lt John Sample. A pre-war auxiliary, Sample went on to serve with the squadron in France, and make several claims whilst leading No 504 Sqn during the Battle of Britain. Given command of newly formed No 137 Sqn in September 1941, he was killed on 28 October when his Westland Whirlwind collided with another twin-engined fighter near Bath (*No 607 Sqn Records*)

on 100 degrees bearing over the North Sea. We saw nor heard anything, so we were told to return. There were banks of broken cloud about 500 ft to one side of us, and we suddenly saw a Do 18 between banks and turned to attack it. The Do 18 went into a dive, levelled off about 50 ft above the water, and then eased its way down to 20 ft, where the pilot nearly put in a wing whilst in a turn. We each attacked in turn from the stern, having no trouble from the rear gunner due to the flying boat's single rudder blocking his view. Fuel was soon pouring from its wing tanks. The Dornier landed after we left, and its crew was picked up by a destroyer, which towed the aircraft until it sank. My aircraft was K8026, letter L.'

Do 18 '8L+DK' of 2./KuFlGr 606, flown by Oberleutnant zur Zee Seigfried Saloga, was the first success for a British Gladiator. The section leader, John Sample, who had been flying K7995/AF-O, made further claims during 1940, being credited with 1 and 2 shared confirmed, 1 and 2 shared probables and 3 damaged.

Occasional Luftwaffe attacks on the Fleet anchorage at Scapa Flow, in the Orkneys, led to the formation of 804 NAS at Hatston under the command of Lt Cdr J C Cockburn, whilst on 28 November, 'B' Flight of No 152 Sqn moved to Sumburgh to defend the Shetlands – in mid-December, the latter became the Fighter Flight Shetland. There were sporadic contacts with the enemy by these small Gladiator units in the northern isles, the first success falling to 804 NAS on 10 April 1940. The unit's diary graphically described the events:

'A tremendous day for HMS *Sparrowhawk* (RNAS Hatston – author), the first, and we hope by no means the last. At 2045 hrs, the evening *blitzkreig* began. Red were scrambled to Copinsay. Yellow 1 (the CO) had the first chase after an e/a (enemy aircraft), which was in a long dive towards Kirkwall, and which peppered Kirkwall and Hatston with its front guns. Red chased after another, and during this party Blue Section came galloping up on seeing the shooting. Plenty of e/a were coming, so "Smee" chose a back one and stuffed himself under its tail. He and his section rattled away with such good effect that the e/a was last seen in a flat right hand spiral going down toward South Ronaldsay.'

Cockburn was credited with one destroyed, whilst Blue Section's claim was assessed as 'damaged'.

The Fighter Flight also had occasional combats. Sqn Ldr Tom Dudley-Gordon, a visiting staff officer, witnessed the events of 18 April:

'One of the pilots sent a wireless message while over the sea that he had got a Heinkel. The successful pilot was a blue-eyed ginger-haired young Scot (Flg Off T W 'Jock' Gillen – author). After he landed, he told me, "I pushed the stick forward, dived down almost vertically and caught the Heinkel's crew by surprise. My first burst of fire probably killed the German air-gunner, for he put up no defence. I turned and put a stream of bullets into one of the Heinkel's engines. A burst of black smoke streamed from it, and it made a gliding descent towards the sea. I followed up the attack until my ammunition had gone, and the Heinkel had disappeared, still losing height".'

Formed in Orkney for the defence of the naval base at Scapa Flow, 804 NAS clashed with the Luftwaffe on several occasions during the spring of 1940. Amongst the aircraft it used during this period was Sea Gladiator N2274, seen here parked at Hatston – note the proximity of the naval anchorage. Vega Gull G-AETF in the background was used for communication flights, and even wears a military fin flash! (*S G Orr*)

Gillen's victim was in fact a Ju 88 that was credited as a probable. He saw more combat on 5 June, as related by the Operational Record Book:

'1430 hrs – Flg Off Gillen intercepted one Do 17 eight miles north of Lerwick at 7000 ft. Flg Off Gillen got on to E/A's tail and gave three bursts before E/A dived through cloud. Flg Off Gillen stayed on E/A's tail and followed. E/A's rear gunner was out of action and engine was on fire. E/A last observed diving vertically towards the sea at 50 ft.'

He was credited with a confirmed kill.

Further south, No 152 Sqn saw action for the first time on 29 January when a He 111 was shot down over Druridge Bay. Its next kill came on 27 February, when Blue Section, including Plt Off Wildblood ('Blue 2') with Plt Off J S Jones as 'Blue 3', was ordered to patrol Farne Island. At 1345 hrs they found the enemy. Wildblood's report takes up the story:

'E/A sighted at 500 ft flying north-east at approximately 200 mph. "Blue 2" attacked immediately on starboard side. After second burst E/A's undercarriage lowered and two streams of white smoke observed from engines. After third burst, E/A dipped and "Blue 2" broke away.

Third from the left, holding a map, is the flight commander of 'B' Flt No 615 Sqn, Flt Lt James Sanders. He is seen briefing his pilots at Vitry-en-Artois before a patrol in the spring of 1940. Sanders had damaged an He 111 in December 1939, and by the time the summer of 1940 was over, he had been credited with the destruction of 16 enemy aircraft (*J G Sanders*)

After another burst "Blue 3" then attacked from starboard side and fired two bursts – during the second, a large portion of starboard engine was observed to fall away. E/A turned steeply to port and flew towards coast. "Blue 3" broke away and remained above E/A until it hit the water. E/A sank in three minutes, with three crew seen to be afloat in a dinghy.'

For 19-year-old Tim Wildblood, this shared victory was the first of

The only claim by an RAF Gladiator in France was made in this aircraft, N2308/KW-T, by 'Sandy' Sanders on 29 December 1939. The Gladiator is seen at Redhill on 22 May 1940, having been evacuated from France by future ace Flg Off Tony Eyre (*F G Swanborough*)

Dispersed in the snow at a very wintry Vitry-en-Artois in February 1940 are aircraft of No 607 Sqn, which formed part of No 60 Wing in support of the BEF. These machines were replaced by Hurricane Is in the spring (*No 607 Sqn Records*)

five successful claims he would make with No 152 Sqn prior to being killed during the Battle of Britain.

In mid-November 1939, No 607 Sqn had joined with No 615 Sqn to form No 60 Wing of the Air Component of the British Expeditionary Force, which then moved to France. They eventually settled at Vitry-en-Artois in muddy conditions, from where patrols were regularly flown. The units only made contact with the Luftwaffe once prior to receiving Hurricanes – a He 111 was intercepted on 29 December by Flt Lt James 'Sandy' Sanders of No 615 Sqn. He remembers:

'I was in aircraft N2308, and took off at 1310 hrs for an "A" patrol. The weather was filthy, and I ended up with frost-bitten fingers. As to the Heinkel, I just couldn't catch it up, but I fired a lot of ammunition at it.'

In the RAF's final combat for 1939, Sanders was awarded a 'damaged' – his only claim with the Gladiator, although he was later credited with 16 kills in Hurricanes during the summer of 1940.

BLITZKRIEG

The German offensive in the West struck with unprecedented ferocity on 10 May 1940, although both Nos 607 and 615 Sqns had, albeit hurriedly, converted to Hurricanes by then. However, other Gladiators were engaged on 10 May, as 15 still served with the *1ère Escadrille de Chasse* ('Le Comete') of the Belgian Army Aviation. At Schaffen, contrary to orders, Capitaine Max Guisgard, commander of 1/I/2, led his biplanes off just ahead of a low-flying attack by He 111s and Do 17s.

Most of Guisgard's aircraft arrived at Beauvechain, from where at 0915 hrs five of them had a one-sided combat with Bf 109s of I./JG 26 and

Amongst the aircraft opposing the Luftwaffe during May 1940 were the Gladiator Is of the *1ère Escadrille de Chasse* of the Belgian *Aeronautique Militare*. Most were either destroyed on the ground or shot down by marauding Bf 109s, this one (which displays the *Escadrille's* 'flaming comet' badge) almost certainly being burnt out on the ground at Beauvechain on 11 May (*F G Swanborough*)

Sgt Pirlot of the *1ère Escadrille de Chasse* relaxes with a cigarette in front of Gladiator I G-19 in July 1939. He subsequently flew this machine into combat with Bf 109Es of I./JG 1 on 11 May 1940. Following a one-sided fight, the biplane fighter fell out of control over the forts at Eban-Emael, with Pirlot probably dead at the controls (*F G Swanborough*)

The only Gladiator unit serving with Fighter Command during the Battle of Britain was No 247 Sqn, based at Roborough for the defence of the Plymouth naval base. It was commanded by Sqn Ldr Peter O'Brien, who flew Mk II N5682/HP-K, seen here in December 1940 shortly before its replacement with a Hurricane I (*P G O'Brien*)

3./JG 27. Three were shot down. Later, others encountered a formation of Ju 87 Stukas, but were quickly set upon by the escorting Bf 109s, and two more fell before the remainder escaped into cloud. The following morning six aircraft, thought to be the only ones remaining, escorted an attack by Belgian Battles against bridges over the Albert Canal. Guisgard, in G-27, led the first section, with 1/Sgt Denis Rolin, in G-22, leading the second.

Over the target they were bounced by Bf 109s from I./JG 1, and in the ensuing fight Rolin probably damaged a fighter before falling to Leutnant Ludwig Franzisket. 1/Sgt Henri Winand, in G-32, claimed one damaged near Sichem. Sgts Pirlot (G-19) and Clinquart were both killed and Guisgard bailed out of his burning aircraft, but later died.

Later that turbulent summer, the Sumburgh Fighter Flight moved to Roborough to become No 247 Sqn for the day and night defence of Plymouth. It was the only Gladiator squadron to serve with Fighter Command during the Battle of Britain, and fortunately it did not encounter the Luftwaffe until 6 November, when at 1915 hrs Plt Off R C Winter damaged an He 111 off Falmouth in the last engagement by a home-based Gladiator. Soon afterwards the unit re-equipped, and the Gladiator passed from operational use in the UK.

ARCTIC WARRIORS

During the autumn of 1939 negotiations over territorial disputes between the Soviet Union and Finland broke down, and on 30 November the Soviets invaded. The 'Winter War' that pitted Soviet might against the Finns, whose plight received much sympathy and support from around the world, had begun.

The small but efficient Finnish Air Force needed additional aircraft with which to oppose the Soviets and, amongst others, on 12 December placed a contract for 30 ex-RAF Gladiator IIs – 20 were purchased, and the rest donated. Given the serials GL-251 to GL-280, the first three were delivered to *Lentolaivue* 26 (LLv 26) on 18 January 1940 and the remainder over the following month. By then, however, the Gladiator had already been blooded in Finnish skies.

Some 55 Gladiators – designated J-8s – had been delivered to the Swedish Air Force (*Flygvapnet*) during the late 1930s, serving with a number of Fighter Wings (*Flygflottilj*). Following the Soviet invasion of its neighbour, the Swedish Air Force raised a volunteer unit, *Flygflottilj* 19 (F 19), comprising an attack squadron of Harts and a fighter squadron of 12 J-8A Gladiators. Commanded by the redoubtable Maj Hugo Becken-hammer, F 19 was ordered to Kemi, in northern Finland, to protect Finnish Lapland, arriving on 10 January 1940.

From here it mounted its first mission on 12 January, when four J-8As led by 2Lt Ian Iacobi escorted four Harts to the Soviet base at Märkäjärvi, where three Polikarpov I-15 fighters were destroyed. During their return flight, two Harts collided and a third was intercepted and shot down by two I-15bis of 145.IAP. The balance was redressed when Iacobi, flying 284/F, destroyed an I-15. He later recounted the event:

'During the approach we escorted the assault flight. When we arrived over Märkäjärvi, we observed parked vehicles and troop columns on the road and concentrations in the village. At the same moment, the Harts

With its dark green camouflage oversprayed with silver to help it blend in better with the snowy landscape of Finland in the winter, ski-equipped J-8A Gladiator 284/K belongs to the Swedish volunteer unit *Flygflottilj* 19. This unit was sent to northern Finland to support the Finns during the Winter War with the Soviets, the outfit including both bomber and fighter elements. It saw action from January to March 1940 (*F G Swanborough*)

J-8A Gladiator 284/F of F 19 was flown by 2Lt Ian Iacobi during the first Swedish mission on 12 January 1940. Patrolling near the unit's Märkäjärvi base, he downed an I-15 that proved to be the first victory credited to the Swedes with the Gladiator over Finland. This aircraft was also used by F 19's most successful pilot, 2Lt Per-Johan Salwen, when he shot down an I-15 on 17 January and an SB-2 bomber on 1 February (*Kari Stenman*)

banked into a dive against observed targets. Now it was our turn. In a dive against vehicle columns on the road east of Märkäjärvi, we dropped our splinter bombs and continued the attack by strafing the road with our machine guns. All of a sudden a horse-drawn sledge blew up – probably filled with ammunition – and the horse with the sledge shafts flew up into the air. A fighter pilot flying behind me had scored a bull's eye, as a result of which the horse was suddenly positioned next to my starboard wings!

'When the attack against the troops and vehicles was over, a few pilots got the opportunity to strafe the enemy airfield at Märkäjärvi. I observed an I-15 banking to the right below us, trying to get into a firing position behind one Gladiator. A short bank to my right put me behind the I-15 before it could fire. I scored a full hit, and the enemy aeroplane half-rolled and crashed into the forest. Just minutes after my recent meeting with the horse, I had experienced another combat "first".'

The Swedish Gladiators next met the Soviets on the 17th, when Beckenhammer led a patrol over the Salle area. Four I-15bis were engaged in a brief combat, and 2Lts Per-Johan Salwen and Martin each shot one down – Soviet pilots Lts Bondarenko and Benediktov were killed and wounded respectively. The next combat took place almost a week later, when Iacobi led a sweep that once again encountered the ubiquitous I-15s. In the subsequent melee, Swedish pilot 2Lt Sjokvist was killed.

The winter of 1939-40 was one of the worst experienced for many years, and it restricted operations to some extent. The Finns, however, were taking a steady and (to the Soviets) unexpected toll of bombers raiding Finnish towns, and these losses continued into February.

On the 1st, several formations of Tupolev SB-2 bombers attacked the road and rail centre of Rovaneimi, and during the second raid they were intercepted by F 19's Gladiators – P-J Salwen shot one bomber down and may have damaged a second.

Meanwhile, LLv 26 was gaining experience with its ex-RAF Gladiator IIs from its Utti base, the unit's two Flights being tasked with the protection of the Kouvola junction.

The conditions endured during the Winter War are self-evident in this photograph, which shows one of F 19's Gladiators being prepared for flight at Kemi in January 1940. Such weather posed many hazards for both sides during the Winter War (*Flygvapnet*)

The first Finnish pilot to claim a kill with the Gladiator was Lt Paavo David Berg, who shot down an I-153 over Hanko on 2 February 1940 during a ferry flight. He would go on to claim a total of 9¹/₂ kills, five of which were scored with the Gladiator. Berg was subsequently shot down and killed flying a Curtiss Hawk 75 during the Continuation War (*Haken Gustavsson*)

Seen at Menaunkangas during mid-February 1940, Gladiator GL-255 was used by Sgt Oiva Tuominen during a remarkable day's action on the 13th of that month when, in one engagement, he brought down three SB bombers and shared in the destruction of a fourth. A few hours later he used this machine to shoot down an R-5 reconnaissance biplane (*Kari Stenman*)

The Gladiator's first action with the Finns came on 2 February when Lt Paavo Berg was ferrying GL-269 from Sweden, where it had been reassembled. Flying over Hanko, he encountered about 20 I-153 fighters, and getting on the tail of one of them, he promptly shot it down before landing at Littoinen, near Turku. Fokker D.XXI pilot Lt 'Joppe' Karhunen of LLv 24 saw him land, and remembers that Berg was very excited by his first kill. He recalls him saying, 'I have shot down a Chaika – it crashed on the ice. My own aircraft has hits, so can I borrow a Fokker so that I can go back and have a look at the wreck?' Berg's own report of his combat with Lt Bedarev of the OIAE reads:

'A squadron of Chaikas bounced me from above. I received several hits to my Gladiator, but a fast evasive turn prevented any further damage. I decided to test the manoeuvrability of my new mount, and the nearest three-aeroplane Chaika section wanted to fight with me. The rest of them flew away.

'The Chaikas made a tight turn to try to finish me off again. I made a turn too, and I discovered that my GL was able to turn with the Chaikas. I had not even warmed up when I was able to get into a firing position behind one of them. I tightened my turn to the extreme, and thus I was able to pull enough deflection, and my short burst hit his engine. The aeroplane I fired at went down on the ice. His comrades decided to turn for home, and my victim made a landing on the ice. The Chaika looked only slightly damaged. I decided to fly back to Littoinen because I feared the hits on my own aircraft might be critical.'

This was the first of Berg's 9¹/₂ victories, of which five were claimed with the Gladiator. This first kill was scored just prior to Danish volunteer Lt Jorn Ulrich claiming a victory for LLv 26. He had scrambled and chased down a DB-3 bomber near Suursaari, on the Gulf of Finland. The man destined to be the leading Finnish Gladiator pilot and, with 44 kills in total, the fifth ranking Finnish ace, Sgt Oiva 'Oippa' Tuominen, also claimed. Flying GL-258, he had engaged the DB-3s escorting I-16s from 149.IAP and in the resulting dogfight had shot one down and evaded the fire of another.

The fight got ever lower until eventually the Soviet pilot tried to break away. The Finn took his chance and hauled the biplane round after him as the chase went on at tree-top height. Slowly gaining, Tuominen got in a killing burst and brought the I-16 down near Kotka. He also claimed one damaged.

A few days later a detachment of nine Gladiators moved to Mensunkangas to cover northern Lake Ladoga, soon followed by another seven covering the north-east of the country from Kuluntalahti.

Gladiator II GL-253 was flown by LLv 26 ace Lauri Lautamaki when he claimed his 2¹/₂ victories on the type. This aircraft saw lengthy service, being finally placed in storage on 18 February 1945 with over 500 flying hours on the airframe (*Kari Stenman*)

The biplane's next kill came on 11 February when another future ace, WO Lauri Lautamäki, brought down an I-16. The next day two SB-2s fell to yet another future ace (with four Gladiator claims) in Cpl Ilmari Joensuu, and Dane Lt Kalmberg. On 13 February the Gladiator enjoyed its most successful day over Finland, when the Mensunkangas detachment engaged several Soviet formations over the frontline. In the afternoon action, one section took on the I-15bis escorts for nine SB bombers. One Polikarpov fell to Joensuu, whilst Ulrich clamed two more – although his Danish colleague Knut Kalmberg was killed. Returning from an uneventful patrol, Lautomaki (in GL-253) and Tuominen (GL-255) met the bombers, now without escorts. The latter's combat report relates the result:

'While on a patrol with WO Lautamäki near Jänisjärvi station, I observed nine SBs east of Soanlahti, heading west. I signalled WO Lautamäki and turned towards the enemy aeroplanes. The formation banked to the east, and east of Soanjoki I caught them and hit the outer SB in the left wing, which burst into flames. The bomber crashed into the forest. Within a minute the next SB had crashed too. The third one also fell, plunging into a small pond.

'Another nine SBs arrived from the direction of Loimola, and they joined up with the previous formation. At first I thought them to be fighters, and kept my distance. But I soon caught them up at Kivijärvi, and attacked the bomber in the outer right position. It started to lose speed. When I fired a second burst, it crashed and burned into the ice on the north shore of Lake Kivijärvi. The enemy shot at me from the ground and scored two hits on my fighter.'

Lautamäki was credited with a half-share in an SB and Tuominen with 3¹/₂ bombers confirmed destroyed. During a later patrol that same day, the latter also downed an R-5 reconnaissance biplane to thus become the first Finnish Gladiator ace. His wingman, Lauri Lautamäki, commented at the time, 'I just wonder how "Oippa" does it. He just squirts once and the bomber is in flames. I have to make several attacks to get the same result!'

The following day both LLv 26 detachments changed their locations, with one moving to Joetseno, and coming under the control of LLv 24. On 15 February a patrol found and attacked a formation of nine DB-3s, one of which was brought down onto the ice at Suulajarvi by Sgt Valio Porvari, a future 7¹/₂-kill ace. Flying GL-264 again in the same area the

The leading Gladiator pilot of the Winter War was Sgt Oiva Tuominen of LLv 26, whose 6¹/₂ victories were accrued during the course of just three combats. He went on to become the fifth ranking Finnish ace of World War 2 with 44 victories to his credit. Tuominen also received Finland's highest military decoration, the Mannerheim Cross (*Kari Stenman*)

next day, he destroyed an I-16 for his second, and final, Gladiator claim – obviously a fan of British biplane fighters, Porvari had scored his first kill flying a Bristol Bulldog! Two evenings later, a mixed force of bombers was intercepted near Kouvola, and Paavo Berg fired on one, hitting it on the port side before it spiralled down to crash near the town. Buoyed by this success, he chased another which he forced down near Virolahti.

The next day – 19 February – Berg's three-aircraft patrol attempted to intercept a bomber formation, but they got tangled up with the escorting I-153s instead and two of them fell to the Gladiators. One was claimed by Berg, who was flying GL-279. He later recounted:

'The Chaika has a back armour plate for the pilot, so firing at them from directly behind with the Gladiator's rifle-calibre guns is useless. Dogfighting them is the best chance to get a Chaika if you are good at it.'

At the controls of GL-279 once again the following day, Berg attacked a formation of 30 SBs over Kouvola, and brought one down to become the second (and last) Finnish Gladiator ace. However, on this occasion he was hit by return fire and forced to bail out. A second bomber, identified as a DB-3, fell to Cpl Joensuu for his third kill.

Since the 1 February action, Soviet bombers had not been seen in F 19's area, although the Swedes had continued to carry out patrols and attacks on targets on the ground. However, at 0845 hrs on the 20th bombers were reported, and 2nd Lts Salwen and Karlsson scrambled to intercept them over Vaala. Salwen brought one down and damaged another, thus making him F 19's top-scoring pilot over Finland. Another DB-3 fell to F 19's guns the next day.

By mid-February, the Finnish Gladiators were being supplanted within LLv 26 by Fiat G.50s, although the Gloster fighter enjoyed one last major combat with the unit. On the 25th Lt Teva's section intercepted a formation of nine R-5 reconnaissance biplanes over the Karelian Isthmus and shot down four of them, two falling to Teva and one to Joensuu for his fourth, and final, Gladiator kill. Antti Joensuu, who later became an officer, was nicknamed 'Pitka-Jim' ('Long Jim') on account of his height, and he 'made ace' the following year flying a G.50. The Soviet escort then intervened and two Gladiators went down.

By now struggling to hold its own in combat, a further four Gloster biplanes were shot down in two combats on the 29th. The second of these engagements had seen the call to scramble come too late, for Soviet I-16s were virtually over the airfield as the Finnish fighters took off. Three Gladiators and a D.XXI were lost in the low-level combat that ensued. In return, a solitary I-16 fell to Sgt Suikanen, which proved to be LLv 26's final claim with the biplane fighter – the surviving Gladiators were transferred to army co-operation squadrons just days later. LLv 26 had flown over 600 sorties with the Gladiator, its pilots claiming 34 Soviet aircraft destroyed for the loss of 11 Gloster fighters in combat and six pilots killed.

In Lapland the Swedes continued in action, even turning back a raid on 24 February with dummy attacks due to frozen guns! They were working on 7 March, however, when a large formation of DB-3s attacked Vaala. The only Gladiator airborne was flown by 2Lt Theler, and he shot down two of them before the faster bombers escaped. He later reported:

'I attacked a formation of three "SBs" and selected the aircraft on the right. This lagged behind the rest of the formation and crashed. I then

CO of No 263 Sqn during both of its expeditions to Norway was Sqn Ldr J W Donaldson. Known as 'Baldy', he was awarded a DSO following the unit's first spell in Scandinavia. Leading his squadron to Narvik in May, he was one of those lost in the sinking of the *Glorious* on 8 June. Donaldson is seen here pre-war with the sister of notable early-war ace James Sanders (*J G Sanders*)

The shattered remains of the Gladiators flown by Sgts Per Waaller (429) and Oskar Lutken (419) bear mute testimony to the effective strafing of the Bf 110 of 1./ZG 76's Oberleutnant Werner Hansen at Fornebu. Waaler had recently landed from a sortie during which he had claimed an He 111 (*Bundesarchiv*)

targeted the left-hand aircraft. It too lost height and crashed. My aircraft was then hit by return fire and the fuel tank damaged, drenching me in fuel, but I was still able to fly on to the forward base at Uleaborg.'

Three days later, on 10 March, F 19 participated in its final combat, and claimed a significant 'scalp'. Six four-engined Tupolev TB-3 heavy bombers raiding the Rovaniemi area were encountered by 2Lt Josef Karlsson. He caught up with them close to the frontier, and concentrating his fire on Sub Lt Karepov's machine (22198), he emptied all his ammunition into it before seeing it crash into the snow behind Finnish lines near the southern end of Lake Kemijarvi. This was the Gladiator's final kill of the 'Winter War', which ended with a ceasefire at 1100 hrs on 13 March.

It's task done F 19 returned to Sweden at the end of the month, its Gladiators having flown 464 sorties and its pilots claiming ten aircraft destroyed in combat for the loss of two.

NORWEGIAN SAGAS

On becoming operational in late 1939, the RAF's No 263 Sqn, which had formed at Filton in October under the command of Sqn Ldr J W 'Baldy' Donaldson, was equipped with 22 Gladiator IIs and a large supply of stores and motor transport to facilitate its designated 'mobile' unit role. It was intended for a secret operation – to reinforce Finland. However, the end of the 'Winter War' led to its return to Filton.

One pilot who arrived at that time was a future eight-victory ace, Plt Off J M V 'Chips' Carpenter, who made several observations on tactics and training to the author:

'When I joined No 263 Sqn at Christmas in 1939, I was just 18. I was so junior, as the saying goes, "if it moves, salute it". "Baldy" Donaldson, the CO, and my flight commander (Flt Lt Stuart Mills – author) were extremely kind in helping me settle into the squadron. A word about the tactics I was taught in early 1940. The best way recommended was to fly in a formation of three aircraft. An enemy bomber was best attacked from below so as to avoid return fire from the rear gunner. In the Gladiator, you did this by diving past the target, pulling up vertically and praying that you and the enemy bomber arrived at the same point at the same time, thus enabling you to shoot him down!

'We were also instructed in how to clear stoppages of the machine guns with one hand, the other being used to fly the aircraft and deal with the enemy. We were given five-minutes' instruction in the classroom!'

The German invasion of Scandinavia – Operation *Weserübung* – met its most serious resistance at Oslo, where the airport at Fornebu was a key target. Based there was the *Jagevingen* (Fighter Wing) of the *Haerens Flygevapen* (Army Air Service), but its only available fighters were seven Gladiators. The Luftwaffe operation began with He 111s flying over Oslo ahead of waves of Ju 52/3m transports, escorted by Bf 110s.

Initial Gladiator patrols had made only brief contact with the Germans, but at 0700 hrs two more, led by Lt Rolf Tradin, took off and flew down Oslo Fjord to patrol over Nesodden. Here, they encountered a large formation below them, and they dived in and attacked the leading wave of Ju 52/3ms. Tradin hit the starboard wing and engine of the aircraft flown by Feldwebel Meier, and it rolled over and crashed near Hovik, killing all on board. Another Ju 52 was attacked by Sgt Waaler, and this may also have crashed. A third aircraft, identified as a 'Do 17' but actually a Bf 110, was attacked near Kolsås by Sgt Kristian Frederik Schye in Gladiator 427. He takes up the story:

'The sky was starting to really fill up with German aircraft. There were plenty of targets, but at the same time I was forced to manoeuvre so as to avoid getting an enemy aircraft behind me. During the dogfight, I flew closer and closer to Fornebu. Suddenly, I saw a German on a reciprocal course some 400-500 metres below me. I cut back the throttle, performed a half-roll and dived straight down on him. I opened fire at a good shooting distance and kept him in my sights until just 50 metres separated us. He then rolled over and disappeared downwards in a spin

Luftwaffe officers examine a surviving Norwegian Gladiator I, which is believed to be aircraft 423. This machine was unserviceable on 9 April, and it therefore played no part in the day's action (*Budesarchiv*)

– later, he was found to have made a forced landing at Wöyenfjordene, near Kolsås, with both engines knocked out.

'Three German aircraft then attacked me, with the third closing in from behind. My left lower wing was hit and perforated, and the fabric on the left side of the cockpit was shot through by splinters. One of these also hit me. I spun down and made a forced landing in a clearing near a small wood, coming to a halt only after I had torn down a high-voltage cable.'

Frederik Schye had shot down the Bf 110 flown by Unteroffizier Helmut Muterscherle, who with his gunner became a prisoner. Schye spent several days in hospital, having himself been the fifth victim of Leutnant Helmut Lent. Another Bf 110, also identified as a Do 17, fell to Lt Dag Krohn, who scored hits around its cockpit – he landed away from base. After this spirited flourish, the *Jagevingen* had been effectively destroyed.

CENTRAL NORWAY

Weserubung led to feverish efforts by the British and French to support the Norwegians. One of the orders issued was for No 263 Sqn to move to provide urgently needed fighter cover to the Anglo-French forces in central Norway around Namsos. One of the flight commanders, Flt Lt Tom Rowland, led the ground party for embarkation in Scotland. In the event, however, delays meant that they never arrived.

On 20 April the CO led 18 Gladiators to Orkney for embarkation aboard the carrier HMS *Glorious*, which sailed on the 22nd. Her own complement included the Sea Gladiators of 802 and 804 NASs. The RAF advanced party had selected the frozen Lake Lesjaskog, between Dombas and Aandalsnes, to house No 263 Sqn, which arrived on the afternoon of the 24th, led by Skuas from 800 NAS. That preparations for the deployment were minimal is evident by these comments from John Carpenter:

'The organisation in Norway was very poor. When we flew off the *Glorious*, we only had one old road map between us. We were supposed to follow a Skua, but I never saw it in the snow storms. None of the groundcrew or armourers belonged to our unit, and they all vanished with

The barrenness of Lake Lesjaskog in central Norway is evident in this view of No 263 Sqn's dispersed Gladiators during the ill-starred first expedition of April 1940. The nearest aircraft – HE-K – wears naval-style camouflage of sky grey sides for the expedition, these having been applied prior to embarkation (*No 263 Sqn Records*)

With effective Luftwaffe attacks being flown at any time during daylight hours, efforts were made to camouflage No 263 Sqn's Gladiators through the use of foliage – note that the Navy Skua behind the Gloster fighter is also covered. Nonetheless, servicing and maintenance facilities were non existent, and only a few patrols flown. Interestingly, although No 263 apparently flew only Gladiator IIs, this machine is fitted with a two-bladed Watts propeller as seen only on the Gladiator I (*No 263 Sqn Records*)

the commencement of the first air raid. The aircraft were refuelled by hand, and the first enemy air attacks broke the ice. When we arrived, we found the senior RAF officer (Wg Cdr Whitney Straight) sitting in the snow trying to belt the ammunition because of the lack of armourers.'

Donaldson's pilots found no facilities, but with hard work in dreadful conditions, two aircraft had been made operational by the following morning. Soon afterwards an attack by an He 111 destroyed four aircraft, and an explosion concussed Donaldson, beginning a day of torment for No 263 Sqn. A later raid by more Heinkels, as well as Ju 88s and Bf 110s, destroyed an additional four Gladiators and six Skuas. By 0900 hrs, a pair of fighters was at last ready to defend the site, and Flt Lt Stuart Mills took off to provide cover. An hour later six more got up, and they covered the troops over the frontline for a full two hours.

During his patrol Mills came across a formation of He 111s and attacked one, being credited with its destruction. In fact the bomber managed to limp back towards Sola, but crashed into the sea during its landing approach. The next patrol, led by Plt Off S R McNamara in N5579, encountered a raid of 12 He 111s and six Ju 88s. On one pass he hit a Heinkel flown by Unteroffizier Nolte, which crash-landed on the lake and burnt out. However, a further attack on Lake Lesjaskog destroyed four more Gladiators, resulting in No 263's position becoming increasingly untenable. Yet despite the raid two more Gladiators got airborne, and over the next two and a half hours engaged in a series of combats over the lake, as Stuart Mills relates:

'After managing to refuel two Gladiators with the aid of two milk jugs acquired from a nearby farm house, I persuaded "Baldy" (flying N5633, with Mills probably in N5641 – author) to join me on a sortie. Six Heinkels which were approaching the lake were driven off by our attacks, and they did not bomb. We then engaged a lone Heinkel, and following a beam attack, we forced the pilot (Feldwebel Hans Gutt of *Stab.*/LG 1 – author) to crash-land the aircraft. We returned to the lake, having been airborne for over two hours. After landing, I gave the order for the squadron to withdraw to Stetnesmoen, some 60 miles away, where "Baldy" had already landed safely.'

From their new base near Aandalsnes, the five survivors flew patrols into the evening. During one flight, the CO intercepted and claimed to have downed a He 111

that was attacking a ship. After a few more sorties the following day, the remaining aircraft were destroyed and the gallant squadron evacuated.

After returning to re-equip with more Gladiators, the CO and Mills were debriefed in London and asked to highlight the many deficiencies during the operation, only to be told by a senior officer, 'You appreciate the squadron was sent to Norway as a token sacrifice.' Amongst the gallantry decorations awarded were a well-earned DSO to Donaldson and a DFC to Mills.

No 263 Sqn was not the only British unit with Gladiators in action off Norway, as both 802 and 804 NASs were busy defending the Navy from Luftwaffe attacks. On 27 April the RN fighters increased their cover over of Aandalsnes in preparation for the evacuation. Their first chance came at 0935 hrs when three aircraft from 804 NAS and one from 802 NAS caught a reconnaissance He 111 of 1(F)./122 low on the water 20 miles from the fleet. Lt Smeeton of 804 led the attack, badly damaging the Heinkel, which eventually crash-landed north-west of Trondheim.

On 1 May, with the evacuation almost complete, the Home Fleet returned to cover the final elements. Luftwaffe efforts intensified to locate the vessels, and a busy day then ensued. Sections of Sea Gladiators

One of the indisputable claims for No 263 Sqn's first expedition was Unteroffizier Helmut Nolte's He 111 of 4./LG 1, which Plt Off McNamara in Gladiator N5579 brought down on 25 April in full view of everyone (*C F Shores*)

During the evacuation of the central Norway expedition Sea Gladiators from 804 NAS, embarked in HMS *Furious*, provided fighter cover over the fleet. One of these aircraft was N2276/H, which was reportedly being flown by Lt Cdr J C Cockburn when he damaged a Ju 87 on 1 May (*R C Sturtivant collection*)

Of the three Gladiators visible in this photograph of Lake Lesjaskog, two are burned out, providing a grim reminder to the squadron of the Luftwaffe's domination of the skies of central Norway in April 1940 (*C F Shores*)

Described by a friend as 'an extraordinarily skilful pilot', Flt Lt Ceasar Hull served with No 263 Sqn during the Narvik expedition. Indeed, he became the RAF's first Gladiator ace after some astounding combats in the Bodo area, before being wounded and evacuated back to England. The Rhodesian was killed during the Battle of Britain (*C F Shores*)

intercepted several raids, including one by six Ju 87Rs of 2./StG 1, which lost the Stuka flown by Oberfeldwebel Erich Stahl – the crew was rescued by a destroyer. It had been brought down by 802 NAS's 'Blue' section off *Glorious*. With the evacuation complete the fleet withdrew to Scapa Flow.

NARVIK EXPEDITION

After its evacuation No 263 Sqn re-equipped with another 18 Gladiator IIs to support the Narvik expedition in northern Norway. This second operation, which was again ultimately futile, witnessed some of the most remarkable individual combats against the odds in the history of the RAF – as well as one of its greatest tragedies.

Work was begun on preparing Bardufoss airfield for No 263 Sqn, and where the long-suffering ground party (still led by Flt Lt Tom Rowland) had moved to after arriving at the port of Harstad on 11 May. The next day the Gladiators were loaded onto HMS *Furious*, which also embarked six aircraft from 804 NAS for her defence. She sailed for Norway three days later in company with *Glorious*, which still carried 802 NAS, as well as the Hurricanes of No 46 Sqn.

No 263 Sqn included several new pilots within its ranks, including Flt Lt Ceasar Hull, who joined from No 43 Sqn, having already scored three shared kills in Hurricanes. *Furious* arrived off Norway on 21 May, but the transit to Bardufoss ended in disaster when two Gladiators crashed into a mountainside in bad weather – one pilot was killed and Flt Lt Mills injured.

The remainder of the squadron flew off in better weather later in the day to be reunited with their groundcrews, as recalled to the author by Tom Rowland. 'On seeing me "Baldy" said "Good God Tom, what are you doing here? Didn't they tell you that you have been posted to No 43 Sqn?"' Tom Rowland's great friend, Ceasar Hull, was his replacement. Of the Rhodesian, Rowland remembers, 'He was the best chap I have ever met – an extraordinarily skilful pilot and a lively character.' However, even as No 263 Sqn was being established, plans for evacuation were already being drawn up because of the desperate situation in France.

The following day No 263 flew over 30 sorties, during one of which Plt Off Craig-Adams (in N5698) either collided or rammed Feldwebel Hess's

He 111. The squadron's first claim had also sadly resulted in its first loss too. However, the following day the remaining aircraft flew in, and during a patrol in the afternoon, Sgt Basil Whall (in N5719) participated in a lengthy combat west of Harstadt, following which he had to bail out due to a shortage of fuel. In his report he recorded:

'I had 1200 ft excess height when I sighted the Dornier (possibly a Bf 110 – author), and made four successive attacks of a quarter deflection type, getting in quite long bursts of approximately four seconds.

'My fire was returned from a four-gun turret on top of the enemy aircraft. My fire appeared to be successful as the Dornier, after using evasive tactics, dived steeply towards the mountains as if hit. I was unable to keep pace with it when my speed dropped off, and I lost sight of it as it neared the ground.'

This, Basil Whall's first claim, was initially not confirmed, but was later included in his total of 7 and 2 shared destroyed. He was killed during the Battle of Britain flying Spitfires with No 602 'City of Glasgow' Sqn.

The next day Flg Off Grant-Ede scrambled and attacked an intruding Bf 110, which he claimed damaged. Later, he intercepted a He 111 over Bardufoss at 500 ft, attacking from the beam and causing damage, whilst Flg Off Bill Riley put out the starboard engine. Hull then appeared and shot out the port engine, and the Heinkel went down. This share was the first of Riley's ten claims before his death in July 1942.

The unit enjoyed more successes on 25 May, and again Grant-Ede was involved. Returning from an early patrol, he encountered a large four-engined aircraft he identified as a 'Ju 90' (it was in fact a Fw 200 V2), and after two short bursts, it went down into the sea. An hour or so later he was airborne again, and encountered another 'Ju 90', which after a lengthy series of attacks, crashed into Finoy Island. Late in the evening a third of these large aircraft was found by Plt Off P H Purdy and Sgt H H Kitchener. The former's handwritten combat report was subscribed with a written note from the CO, Sqn Ldr Donadson: 'Aircraft found, and so this was a confirmed victory'. Of this combat, Kitchener, in correspondence specially for this volume, recalled the combat as lasting five minutes

'My section leader, Plt Off Purdy, and I were on patrol in search of an enemy seaplane in the Harstadt area. On Purdy's signal I sighted a "Junkers 90". I attacked within ten seconds of Purdy, and kept up an attack, firstly from its port quarter and then from directly astern, for nearly five minutes, using short bursts. Approximately four miles off Sorreissa it struck the water.'

To destroy three such large aircraft in one day was a significant feat for the Gladiators, which were to enjoy more success the next day. Mid-morning, Flt Lt Alvin Williams, a Canadian, shared in the destruction of a 'Ju 88' (actually a Do 17F) with Sgt Milligan – it was the first of six victories (five of them shared) for Williams. Later, two other pilots, led by Bill Riley, attacked further bombers over Harstad. Just prior to this action taking place, Ceasar Hull, Plt Off Falkson and Lt Tony Lydecker RN had been detached to a hastily prepared landing ground at Bodo, at the southern end of Vestfjord. The operating conditions there were primitive, and the landing surface was a sea of mud. Hull's diary recorded:

'The Wing Commander explained that the Army was retreating up a valley east of Bodo and was being strafed by the Huns all day. Sounded too easy, so I took off just as another Heinkel 111 circled the aerodrome. God! What a take-off! Came unstuck about 50 yards from the end and just staggered over the trees. Jack (Falkson) followed and crashed. Saw some smoke rising, so investigated and found a Heinkel 111 at about 600 ft. Attacked it three times, and it turned south with smoke pouring from fuselage and engines. Broke off attack to engage a Junkers 52, which crashed in flames. Saw Heinkel 111 flying south, tried to intercept, and failed. Returned and attacked two Junkers 52s in formation. Number one went into clouds, number two crashed in flames after six people had bailed out. Attacked Heinkel 111 and drove it south with smoke pouring from it. Ammunition finished, so returned to base.'

The two Gladiators at Bodo covered shipping evacuating the port through the night, then it was time to depart. However, things then went wrong, as Hull's diary graphically describes:

'Suddenly at 0800 hrs the balloon went up. There were 110s and 87s all around us, and the 87s started dive-bombing a jetty about 800 yards from the aerodrome. Tony's aircraft started at once and I waved him off, then after trying mine a bit longer I got yellow, and together with the fitter made a dive into a nearby barn. From there we watched the dive-bombing in terror until it seemed that they were not actually concentrating on the aerodrome.

'Got the Gladiator going and shot off without helmet or waiting to do anything up. Circled the 'drome climbing, and pinned an 87 at the bottom of a dive. It made off slowly over the sea (the aircraft, flown by Feldwebel Kurt Zube of 1./StG 1, crashed into the sea – author) and just as I was turning away, another 87 shot up past me, and his shots went through my windscreen, knocking me out for a while. Came to, and was thanking my lucky stars, when I heard rat-tat behind me and felt my Gladiator hit. Went into right hand turn and dive, but could not get it out. Had given up hope at 200 ft, when she centralised, and I gave her a burst of engine to clear some large rocks. Further rat-tats from behind, so gave up hope and decided to get her down. Held off then crashed.'

Ceasar Hull had been brought down wounded in the head and knee by Bf 110 ace Helmut Lent, and because of his injuries he was evacuated

One of the few surviving photographs of No 263 Sqn at Bardufoss shows Gladiator II N5626 in standard Fighter Command colours, but wearing no unit codes. In the wake of the first disastrous expedition, the unit had been hastily re-equipped, although official records fail to show that this particular machine ever served with the squadron! (*No 263 Sqn Records*)

back to England via Harstad, where he met up with his friend Tom Rowland. Lydecker, meanwhile, had also been heavily hit, but he managed to reach Bardufoss in his wrecked biplane. Hull's successes over the previous days made him the RAF's first Gladiator ace, and its most successful pilot of the Norwegian campaign. He subsequently returned to No 43 Sqn upon his recovery, and led the unit until he was killed in a dogfight over London on 7 September 1940.

No 263 Sqn's Gladiators had further encounters on succeeding days as May came to an end, with a He 111 of KG 26 being destroyed over Ofotfjord by Flt Lt Alvin Williams (in N5681) for his second victory – Oberleutnant Streng and his crew were rescued by German troops. That same day – 28 May – Glorious's Sea Gladiators from 802 NAS were also in action, when a section led by Lt G H Feeny downed a He 115 floatplane of 2./KuFlGr 506, which broke up upon hitting the water. This was 802 NAS's final victory. The relative lull of the next few days allowed both Nos 46 and 263 Sqns time to recover, as well as to conduct some ground attack sorties in support of the Army.

On 2 June the order to evacuate Norway led to increased Luftwaffe efforts, which in turn resulted in two remarkable combats being fought by No 263 Sqn. The cover over Narvik was limited by its distance from the unit's Bardufoss base, so in the early afternoon Plt Off Louis Jacobsen took off with Plt Off Wilkie to patrol near the Swedish border. They came across two Bf 110s, and Wilkie fell to the guns of Helmut Lent before the Messerschmitt fighters dived away into cloud.

Realising he was in Swedish airspace, Jacobsen had just started to turn back towards Norway when sighted more enemy aircraft, which he promptly attacked. One 'He 111' (probably a Do 17 of 4(F)./ObdL) reared up after being hit in the cockpit, and it crashed onto the barren Bjornfell. Jacobsen was then attacked by other 'Heinkels' and Bf 110s, and he fired as the opportunity arose, although his aircraft was sustaining damage all the time. With his windscreen covered in oil he fired off his last ammunition at a 'He 111' in front of him, and with its engines on fire it glided down whilst Jacobsen limped back to base.

His remarkable combat against the odds saw him credited with four destroyed, but other aircraft found inside Sweden may also have been downed as a result of his fire. Whatever the actual result, this remarkable single-handed combat resulted in the immediate award of the DFC to the 25-year-old New Zealander.

At 1500 hrs another patrol took off, and south of Narvik Flt Lt Williams and Sgt Kitchener met 12 He 111s. The latter pilot wrote of the subsequent events:

'I took off in Gladiator N5905 (coded HE-N – author) to patrol Narvik district. After becoming airborne, I observed four He 111s in formation 2000 ft above me. After about three minutes, with Flt Lt Williams, I attacked the formation. The He 111s proceeded to dive. Between us, we caught up the straggling Heinkel. I attacked from the beam, Flt Lt Williams from astern. Both engines and the fuselage caught alight, and the aircraft dived out of control and crashed. We then caught up with the next straggler, and a similar attack was carried out. Both engines caught alight, and it subsequently crashed. Both these aircraft can be found between five and twenty miles respectively north-east of Narvik.

Although taken after the Norwegian campaign, this dramatic photograph shows well the 'arrival' of a Sea Gladiator on the deck of an aircraft carrier – something which required slick action, especially during Luftwaffe air attacks (*author's collection*)

'For the next 20 minutes, between the two of us, we carried out seven more attacks of a similar nature. Both engines of the third Heinkel in formation were put out of action, and it was seen to be diving out of control to the ground. We then both attacked a Ju 87 – it was one of two, and had a large extra tank beneath each side of the mainplanes about four feet from the wingtip. This aircraft put up strong resistance, but the port tank caught alight and the aircraft crashed into the top of a hill some 30 miles south of Narvik (this Ju 87R was from 2./StG 1, flown by Oberleutnant Bohne, who was killed – author).

'I observed Flt Lt Williams closing on a He 111 which was bobbing in and out of clouds. I was unable to catch up at the time, as while I was getting into position a Ju 87 crossed my sights and so I attacked. When I had finished with it, a white stream of smoke was coming from the engine, and I lost it in cloud. Further attacks were made, but no definite results can be claimed. I returned to base having run out of ammunition.'

The pair were credited with three He 111s and a Ju 87 shared destroyed, whilst Alvin Williams claimed another He 111, which was unconfirmed, and Kitchener a Stuka damaged. On 6 August (the same day that Herbert Kitchener's DFM was promulgated) the posthumous award of the DFC to Alvin Williams was made – a singularly rare occurrence, as such posthumous awards were not normally made.

The squadron then continued operations during a period of adverse weather whilst preparations for the evacuation of Narvik proceeded. Patrols continued on 7 June prior to their embarkation on *Glorious*, followed in the early hours of 8 June by the Hurricanes of No 46 Sqn. No 263 Sqn's achievements were considerable, for in 13 days of flying it had engaged in some 72 individual combats, claiming at least 26 victories, and possibly as many as 35 – only two Gladiators were known to have been lost in combat.

Having fought successfully against the odds, it was a tragic irony that later that day *Glorious* and her escorts were engaged and sunk by the German battlecruisers *Scharnhorst* and *Gneisenau* with the loss of 1,519 lives, including the whole of No 263 Sqn and 802 NAS. Of the loss of the squadron in the *Glorious*, Flt Lt Stuart Mills later wrote:

'So poor "Baldy" and my young and gallant friends, who had done so wonderfully well at Bardufoss with their slow aeroplanes against Heinkels and Junkers 87s and 88s, had a dreadful end.'

THE DESERT AND MALTA

Flg Off John Lapsley, in K8011/YK-S, tucks in on his leader during a formation practice flight over Egypt in the spring of 1940. Upon the outbreak of war, he flew with No 80 Sqn's Hurricane flight, which later became No 274 Sqn. Lapsley would shoot down three S.79s in one combat, and by the end of 1940 had claimed 11 victories (*J H Lapsley*)

The Italian declaration of war on 10 June 1940 found all of the RAF's Egyptian-based fighter squadrons – No 33 at Mersa Matruh, 80 at Amriya and 112 at Helwan, as well as No 94 in Aden – eager to prove their superiority over the *Regia Aeronautica*. Forward-based, No 33 Sqn duly conducted the first war patrols with its Gladiators on the 11th, but nothing untoward was seen.

The third RAF Gladiator unit to see action over the desert was No 112 Sqn, which initially provided a detachment that operated alongside No 33 Sqn. Three of its pilots pose in front of K6142/RT-U in early 1940, but unfortunately their identities remain unrecorded (*C Williams*)

In order to be closer to the front, No 33 Sqn moved six Gladiators forward to Sidi Barrani on the 13th, and from there the following morning three fighters flew an offensive patrol as far west as Bardia. Flg Off E H 'Dixie' Dean, in N5782, and Plt Off Vernon Woodward (N5783) took off at 0955 hrs, followed by Sgt Craig (N5768), on a sortie which one hour later began the air fighting of the long desert campaign. Ernest 'Dixie' Dean recounts the historic encounter:

'Soon after being promoted to flying officer, I was posted to No 33 Sqn at Mersa Matruh. I had a good flight with Verne Woodward, Peter Wickham and Sgt Craig. It wasn't long after Italy declared war that we were moved to Sidi Barrani. We had no warning system at all of aircraft movement by the enemy, and only very sketchy and vague locations of both ours and their positions from the Army. We carried out the old traditions of patrolling along and over the border in the beginning in "vics" and pairs. Later, we flew bigger sweeps with more aircraft.

The first enemy aircraft to be shot down during the desert campaign fell to Flg Off E H Dean of No 33 Sqn on 14 June 1940. Flying this particular Gladiator (N5782), he destroyed a CR.32 near Fort Capuzzo. The aircraft was later passed on to No 3 Sqn RAAF, whose pilots also used it to destroy several Italian aircraft (*V Fordyke*)

'The combat of 14 June near Fort Capuzzo was our very first encounter with the enemy. An inoffensive-looking light bomber was seen, and I detached Woodward and Sgt Craig to attack, whilst I stayed aloft to cover. Within a short spell I saw six aircraft in line astern heading from the west. I recognised them as CR.32s. I remember being quite calm, and wondering what the heck to do. I flew towards them, keeping them well to my right – with the thought of getting behind them (and shooting them down one by one – silly boy!).

'Before I got close enough to them, they split in all directions and formed a ring around me – the sitting duck! I remembered somewhere about flying extraordinarily badly to present a very bad target. I throttled back, yawed and waffled up and down and around, and could hear the thump of their half-inch cannon at each pass, and as each came into my sights having a rapid squirt at them. This seemed to go on for ages, and eventually one of them dropped away and suddenly the remainder disappeared, and I was thankfully alone in the sky and flew back.

Whilst returning to Amriya following a night flight on 26 March 1940, Plt Off G T Baynham suffered a loss of power during an attempted overshoot and hit the ground. K7973/YK-Y was later repaired, whilst Baynham eventually returned to the UK, where he shot down seven German aircraft between 1941 and 1943 (*J H Lapsley*)

Flg Offs Ernest Dean (second from right) and Vernon Woodward (second from left) participated in the RAF's first combat over the desert. In addition to Dean's CR.32, Woodward shared in the destruction of a Ca.310 bomber. On the left is Sgt Slater, who on 25 July downed a CR.42 and shared another with Woodward, whilst on the right is Flg Off A R Costello, who claimed at least one confirmed victory after joining No 112 Sqn
(*Wg Cdr E H Dean*)

'I heard upon my return to base at debriefing that one CR.32 (an aircraft of 8° *Gruppo*, flown by Sergente Edoardo Azzaroni who was killed – author) had been destroyed, apparently by me, whilst Woodward and Craig had shared the bomber (a Caproni Ca.310 of 159ª *Squadriglia*, 12° *Gruppo*, flown by Sergente Maggiore Stefano Garrisi). I did hear later that the pilot of the CR.32 had been struck by a single bullet through the heart.'

This was the first of five victories for Dean, whilst Woodward would be credited with a further 17 kills with No 33 Sqn over the next year. The unit subsequently found it hard to intercept the faster Italian bombers, especially the Savoia S.79, but air combats nevertheless became more frequent, with a number of future aces beginning to score. One was Flg Off Peter Wickham of No 112 Sqn (on loan to No 33), who on 19 June claimed a CR.32 and an Ro.37 reconnaissance biplane near Sidi Aziez.

Ten days later, during a patrol over Fort Capuzzo, three Gladiators had engaged an equal number of CR.32s, and 'Woody' Woodward despatched those of SottoTen Weiss and Ten Buliarini. The run of success continued on the 30th near Bardia, when both Wickham and Dean claimed. The latter describes the action:

'Peter Wickham and I were patrolling near Bardia, and spotted two CR.42s. We each took one, and within minutes there were two black plumes on the ground. I got involved with another CR.42, a quite aggressive "Eyetie" (most rare), and I unfortunately got into head-on attacks with him, which are not recommended. We had three passes at one another but with no apparent damage, except that when we reached base together I didn't perform any victory rolls, although Pete was performing perfect flick rolls in formation. Lucky for me, because my riggers reported to me that my centre section was badly damaged, and it was well I had overcome my exuberance.'

The following day another leading Gladiator alumni began to score when Sgt Bill Vale – nicknamed 'Cherry' – shot down a CR.32 over Capuzzo. Taking off in N5769 at 1145 hrs on his third sortie of the day, his logbook laconically records 'Patrol Sidi Barrani – Capuzzo. 1 F 32'. A pre-war regular, Vale was very experienced, and by the time this action took place he had over 700 flying hours to his name.

4 July also saw more success for No 33 Sqn when two CR.42s were brought down, one of which fell to Flt Sgt Len Cottingham in N5779 (the first of his eventual 11 1/2 victories). That evening, whilst patrolling over Monastir, near Bardia, a formation that included four of the attached No 112 Sqn pilots added to the day's 'bag'. Nine CR.42s of 2° *Stormo* were spotted taking off, so one section that included Flg Off Anthony Gray-Worcester dived after them, and in an astonishing combat he shot down four of them! Others joined the fray, and two more fell to Len Cottingham in N5765.

Claims totalled nine destroyed, and the Italians recorded six lost and four badly damaged. Cottingham also claimed an S.79 in the engagement. Sadly, the promising Gray-Worcester was killed in an accident two weeks later.

No 80 Sqn, meanwhile, still remained in the rear on defensive duties, but when it was finally called into action on 4 July, Plt Off 'Sam' Weller and Flg Off 'Shorty' Graham chased a formation of ten SM.79s north of Alexandria, claiming one probable.

One of No 112 Sqn's Gladiator Is comes to grief in mid-1940, shortly before the squadron moved into the desert in July for action against the Italians. Several of its pilots would begin their route to acedom in summer clashes (*author's collection*)

The following day, No 80 Sqn's new CO arrived. Sqn Ldr Paddy Dunn (later Air Marshal Sir Patrick) told the author of his first trip with No 80:

'I recall my first trip in the Gladiator well. Having been appointed to command No 80 Sqn, I had not flown a Gladiator before, although I had of course flown a Gauntlet. On this first trip the engine stopped, and although I had never landed one, I now had the whole of the Western Desert on which to do so!'

In the desert No 112 Sqn, minus 'B' Flight, which was detached to the Sudan, moved up to Gerawala to support No 33, which lost a Gladiator to CR.42s on 23 July. The unit gained its revenge the following day when, in a fight with 18 CR.42s of 10° and 13° *Gruppi*, it claimed four, including one to Vernon Woodward, who also scored a probable.

'B' Flight was in action the following evening when it encountered seven CR.42s whilst escorting Blenheims over Bardia. Five were claimed, with Vernon Woodward downing one and sharing another with Sgt Slater. The latter was then shot down, and Woodward had a torrid time before he was able to disengage and return home. These were the last of his 4 and 2 shared kills with the Gladiator, and also the last for No 33 Sqn, which on 1 August was replaced forward by 'B' Flight of No 80 Sqn.

The new unit's first serious combat came in the late afternoon of 4 August, when four Gladiators escorted a Lysander on a reconnaissance of Italian positions in the Bir Taieb el Esem area, 30 miles inside the Libyan border. Led by the flight commander, Flt Lt 'Pat' Pattle, in K7910, the patrol comprised Flg Off Johnny Lancaster with Flg Off Peter Wykeham-Barnes and Sgt Kenneth Rew in the second section.

As they neared the target the Lysander was threatened by enemy aircraft. These were seven Breda Ba.65 attack bombers of El Adem-based 159° *Squadriglia*, led by Capt Antonio Dell 'Oro. Escorting them were CR.32s of 160° *Squadriglia*, led by Capt Duilio Fanali.

Aces in waiting! Three of No 80 Sqn's most notable pilots are seen in this photograph, taken at Amriya just before the outbreak of war with Italy. They are 'Tap' Jones (on the left), 'Pat' Pattle (in the centre) and Peter Wykeham-Barnes (on the right). Between them they were to claim over 70 victories, of which around 50 were credited to Pattle, thus making him the most successful Commonwealth fighter pilot by some margin (*E G Jones*)

No 80 Sqn's first victory with Gladiators was claimed by Flg Off Wykeham-Barnes on 4 August 1940 in this aircraft (L8009/YK-I) when he brought down a Ba.65 and a CR.32, before being forced to bail out. By the time he joined No 274 Sqn upon its formation in mid-August 1940, he had claimed 3^1/$_2$ Gladiator victories (*E G Jones*)

Wykeham-Barnes dived on four Bredas, attacking the left-hand aircraft, which spiralled down in flames to become No 80 Sqn's first Gladiator kill. Rew went for the right-hand Breda, but was attacked by the Fiats and shot down by Capt Fanali. Wykeham-Barnes, too, was soon embroiled with the CR.32s, and after downing one, he was severely hit by Mar Romolo Cantelli and forced to bail out. Pattle then dived to engage. He wrote at the time:

In the spring of 1940, Gladiator I L8011/YK-O was the personal mount of No 80 Sqn's 'B' Flight commander, Flg Off 'Pat' Pattle. Seen at Amriya, it remained with the squadron until passed on to the Royal Hellenic Air Force in December of that same year (*E G Jones*)

'I was leading the top flight of Gladiators and dived down to investigate as I did not see the E/A. Whilst in the dive, I heard Flg Off Wykeham-Barnes over the R/T lead his section to the attack, and immediately afterwards saw seven Breda 65s (one flight of four and one of three) flying west just behind the Lysander. Flg Off Wykeham-Barnes attacked the formation of four, so I selected the remaining three and delivered an astern attack. The Bredas turned through 360 degrees and again headed west. This enabled me to get to about 300 yards behind them. I held my fire, hoping to close in still further, and at this time noticed that Plt Off Lancaster, who was on my left, had broken away.

'The Bredas dropped to about 200 ft and released two bombs each, which judging from the burst resembled our own 20 pounders. This was done probably to increase their speed, and also to affect my aim. Their speed in fact did increase, and I was just about to break away when they turned north for El Adem. Turning inside them, I closed to about 150 yards and delivered a quarter attack on the nearest Breda. On the first burst both my port guns ceased to fire. The Breda, however, had been hit, for after a few more bursts from dead astern, white smoke poured out of the starboard side of the engine and it force-landed satisfactorily on good ground five miles further on.

'I then broke away and attempted without result to clear my port fuselage gun. I was then immediately attacked by five Fiat CR.42s, who were flying about 2000 ft above me, and coming from the direction of El Adem, which was approximately ten miles to the north-west. A dogfight ensued in which they made repeated attacks, simultaneously from the quarter and beam, using the speed they gained in the dive to regain altitude after each attack. My own tactics were mainly defensive, turning away from each attack and delivering a short attack on the most suitable target as it dived past.

'On one occasion a Fiat, on completing its attack, turned round in front of my aircraft, presenting an excellent deflection shot at close range. I fired a long burst and it turned slowly on its back and spun towards the ground. I last saw it spinning at 200 ft. Shortly afterwards my starboard wing gun packed up, but the Fiats broke away at the same time. My position was then five miles west and a few miles north of Bir Taieb el Essem.

'I then turned back for the border, but on approaching El Essem I was again intercepted by 12 Fiats and 3 Bredas. The Bredas, after a few dives, broke away, but the Fiats carried out exactly the same tactics as the earlier five. On my first burst the remaining gun jammed as a result of an exploded round in the breech, so I attempted to make the border by evasive tactics and heading east whenever possible. After a running fight lasting approximately 15 minutes, my rudder controls were shot away. No longer able to use evasive tactics, I bailed out after climbing to 400 ft, and landed about four miles inside the border at about 1900 hrs.'

The engagement described so analytically here was the first of about 50 successes claimed by Pattle, who like Wykeham-Barnes was picked up the following day by patrols of the 11th Hussars. Lancaster was wounded but managed to crash-land at Sidi Barrani. As alluded to by Sir Patrick Dunn to the author, reasserting the RAF's superiority was vital:

'My first combat in a Gladiator was on 8 August 1940 when I flew K8009. Having lost four chaps shot down four days earlier – Wykeham-Barnes, Pattle etc – we needed to get back right away and stop the "Eyeties" getting their tails up. And of course, we had to get our own back. It was a planned operation, and it went frightfully well.

'We saw the "Eyeties" from a long way out, and we managed to stay in the sun and close in to around 200 yards before opening fire. My number two (I forget his name), who was on my right, disappeared, however. I have no idea what happened to him, as the sky was full of falling aircraft and parachutes, although I do not believe he went down in flames as has been reported elsewhere.'

No 80 Sqn, reinforced by Dunn, who had earlier led 'C' Flight forward, did indeed inflict a significant reverse on the Italians when they attacked the 16 CR.42s of 9° and 10° *Gruppi*, which were escorting Ro.37s. Pattle's combat report offers an insight into this highly successful engagement:

'I was leading the top section of three aircraft in a formation of 13 Gladiators which took off from our base at 1740 hrs. The formation crossed the border at approximately 1800 hrs at Sidi Omar. At 1825 hrs, when approaching Bir El Gobi,

Instigator of the planned, and very successful, engagement by Gladiators of No 80 Sqn on 8 August 1940 was unit CO Sqn Ldr Paddy Dunn. He scored his only Gladiator victories during the course of the day, downing two CR.42s. Dunn left soon afterwards to form No 274 Sqn, where he enjoyed further successes (*C F Shores*)

a large formation of 27 CR.42s were sighted at about 6000 ft on the starboard beam, flying east.

'Our formation wheeled to attack and approached the enemy formation from the east, the first section approaching within range unobserved. Immediately the first section engaged, the enemy formation split up and a general dogfight followed. I saw Nos 2 and 3 sections engage, and before I brought my section into the fight I saw five crashed aircraft on the ground, three of which were in flames. My own section then engaged those E/A who were attempting to reach their own base, and immediately became engaged in separate combats.

'I engaged a CR.42 and, after a short skirmish, got into position immediately behind him. On firing two short bursts at about 50 yards' range, the E/A fell into a spin and burst into flames on striking the ground. The pilot did not abandon his aircraft. I then attacked 3 E/A immediately below me. This action was indecisive, as after a few minutes they broke away by diving vertically for the ground and pulling out at low altitude.

'Whilst searching for other E/A, I saw two more aircraft crash and burst into flames. Owing to the widespread area, and the number of aircraft engaged, it was impossible to confirm what types of aircraft were involved in these crashes, or who shot them down. The sky seemed clear of '42s, although several Gladiators were still in the vicinity. I was about to turn for our base when a '42 attacked me from below. With the advantage of height, I dived astern of him and, after a short burst, he spun into the ground in flames. As before, the pilot did not abandon his aircraft. Flg Off Graham confirms both my combats, which ended decisively.'

In this sharp five-minute combat, nine CR.42s were claimed destroyed, with six more probables. The CO was credited with two of his eventual 6 and 3 shared total, whilst both Pattle (flying K7971) and Wykeham-Barnes avenged the events of the 4th, with the former shooting down two Fiats and the latter one. Another opening his score on this day was Plt Off Sid Linnard, who claimed two of his 6$^{1}/_{2}$ total, as did Plt Off 'Heimer' Stuckey, who was credited with two and a probable of his 5$^{1}/_{2}$ total, all scored with the Gladiator.

In a final moving comment on the day, Sir Patrick Dunn stated that 'We were not heroes, but just got on with the job in hand.'

These events obviously discouraged the Italians, for No 80 Sqn's next action did not take place until 17 August, when it provided cover for warships returning from a raid on Bardia. Flying just off the Libyan coast at 0820 hrs, Wykeham-Barnes (in K8051) and Flg Off 'Keg' Dowding downed a Cant Z.501 flying boat into the sea. Later that morning a patrol from 'A' Flight No 112 Sqn, led by Canadian Flt Lt 'Algy' Schwab, continued the task.

After seeing bursts of anti-aircraft fire from the fleet, the patrol spotted about 25 S.79 bombers attacking their charges. The first group were

Another ace to claim his first victories on 8 August was Plt Off Sid Linnard, who is seen here sat in his Gladiator K8017 – note his personal motif below the cockpit. Of the nine CR.42s claimed that day, Linnard was credited with two. He made further claims over Greece, but his next confirmed victory was not until December 1941 (*C F Shores*)

After pulling out of the desert, No 33 Sqn settled at Helwan, where Flg Off Vernon Woodward is seen in Gladiator N5784/NW-L during September 1940. He began flying Hurricanes with the squadron soon afterwards, and served with it in Greece (*V C Woodward*)

Regarded as quiet on the ground, in the air 'Woody' Woodward was a veritable tiger! He was one of No 33 Sqn's leading lights, and within a year had been credited with over 20 victories, including 4¹/2 with the Gladiator (*V C Woodward*)

driven off before Schwab led an attack on another five, one of which he shot down. Plt Off Peter Wickham, who had previously been attached to No 33 Sqn, led his section against a third formation, and he too destroyed one for his final Gladiator kill. Further S.79s were claimed by other British fighters.

By the end of the month, with the Italians massing on the Egyptian border, it was evident that an offensive was imminent. On 1 September No 80 Sqn's 'B' Flight moved east to Sidi Haneish, having been replaced at Sidi Barrani on the 3rd by No 112 Sqn's 'A' Flight. Initially, things remained quiet, although 'Heimer' Stuckey claimed his third kill (an S.79) over Barrani on the 10th. The Italian invasion began on the 13th, so the unit withdrew to Sidi Haneish where, two days later, it was joined by the rest of No 80 Sqn.

The ponderous Italian advance soon stopped 'to consolidate', and on the 15th ten S.79s attempted to attack Sidi Barrani again. A section of No 80 Sqn Gladiators attacked one group, but lost a fighter to crossfire. No 112 Sqn they hit the intruders from above, damaging two. From then on Gladiator units experienced only sporadic action, although bomber escorts were often flown. Also at this time, a new Gladiator unit came into being when 'A' Flight of No 33 Sqn passed its aircraft to No 3 Sqn RAAF, which had initially arrived in-theatre as an army co-operation unit.

On 9 October, a lone patrol conducted by No 80 Sqn new boy Plt Off R N 'Ape' Cullen came across a formation of Ba.65s. He attacked,

Seen at Helwan in October 1940, this machien was one of No 33 Sqn's last Gladiators. It was duly passed as partial equipment to No 3 Sqn RAAF, which also operated Gauntlet and Lysander flights. The unit soon made its mark as a fighter squadron, however, and eventually became fully Gladiator equipped (*K Isaacs*)

probably destroying one – the aircraft was last seen losing height trailing a thick plume of smoke. For the charismatic and aggressive Cullen, this was the first of seven claims with the Gladiator out of an overall total of 15$^{1}/_{2}$.

No 33 Sqn's last Gloster fighter departed on 26 October, and the biplane's next large combat occurred five days later. On the afternoon of the 31st, No 112 Sqn engaged 15 S.79s and 18 CR.42s over British forward positions in a combat of mixed fortunes. Two Gladiators fell to the Italians, but 'Algy' Schwab led 2Lt Smith and Plt Off Acworth into the escorts. Schwab destroyed two Fiats and Acworth one, for the first of his 4$^{1}/_{2}$ Gladiator 'kills'. However, he and Smith then collided and both were forced to bail out.

Two days prior to this action taking place, the Italians had invaded Greece, and the RAF was required to support the Greeks. As a result, three Blenheim units and No 80 Sqn were ordered across the Mediterranean – the latter left Egypt in mid-November. On the 2nd of the month No 3 Sqn RAAF had moved its flights of Gauntlets and Gladiators (the third flight had Lysanders) forward to Gerawla, from where operations began on the 13th.

AUSTRALIAN DEBUT

On 18 November Schwab, by now a flight commander, took off to intercept a lone S.79, which be engaged and brought down for his fourth victory. The following day, however, belonged to the eager Australians. Their first combat with the *Regia Aeronautica* resulted in an epic fight when four Gladiators engaged 18 Fiat CR.42s. Flt Lt Pelly, in N5753, had taken off in the early afternoon to perform a recce mission, escorted by Sqn Ldr Heath and Flg Offs Rawlinson (L9044/NW-Z) and A H Boyd (N5752/NW-G).

Heading for the target area at 5,500 ft, they spotted around a dozen CR.42s strafing British ground positions. The Gladiators were engaged by the Italians, and Pelly, who was in the lead, quickly found himself involved with nine of the Fiats. A similar sized group took on the other three. Attacked from behind by a trio of Fiats, Alan Boyd manoeuvred violently and soon found himself behind one of them. He fired a long burst into the cockpit area and the Fiat rolled over and dived into the ground. He then pulled into a tight turn, and in a quarter attack brought his guns to bear on another CR.42. This one too fell into an uncontrolled spin, with thick black smoke pouring from the engine.

Without pause, Boyd swung round after a third Fiat, which was attacking one of the other Gladiators, and it fell away after he had fired a short burst into it. He was then attacked by another, and pulling back with full power, he climbed vertically and the Fiat overshot. Boyd then attacked another in spite of his guns having jammed. He desperately attempted to unblock them – all this whilst being chased at low level over the desert. Having freed up his fuselage guns, Boyd pulled into a loop, which resulted in him being positioned above and behind the Italian, who was now less that 30 yards away. He fired and saw strikes all over the cockpit as it fell into the desert. There were no more CR.42s in his vicinity.

In the distance Boyd saw Pelly being attacked by two Fiats, so he fired at the closer and it dived toward the desert from a height of only 30 ft. Pelly, with a faltering engine, climbed away whilst Boyd, desperately short of ammunition, was chased at very low level for a mile or so by the remaining Fiat. He then rejoined Pelly, whose engine eventually gave out, so he force-landed at Minqar Qaim. Thus Alan Boyd returned to Gerawala alone.

The engagement had lasted for some 25 minutes, with the Australians losing Sqn Ldr Heath, who was later buried next to the remains of his aircraft. In return, however, Boyd was credited with three Fiats destroyed, one probable and two damaged, whilst Rawlinson claimed two damaged. Pelly scored one destroyed and one damaged, and later wrote:

'While proceeding on a reconnaissance to Sofafi area in company with an escort of three other Gladiators, I encountered two formations of CR.42 aircraft consisting of eight and nine respectively. The formation of eight attacked my escort, and the other formation cut me off and drove me southwards. The interception occurred at 1400 hrs when I was seven miles East of Rabia, and my escort two miles north-east of me. I was at 4000 ft and my escort at 5000 ft.

'I could not get back to my escort, and the repeated attacks of the nine CR.42s forced me southwards, and I worked eastwards. Shortly after the commencement of the battle, I found myself meeting one E/A head on at 50 ft. We both opened fire, and he dived under me and crashed.

'About five E/A must have broken off, but at least three pursued me and attacked determinedly until 1425 hrs, when I worked northwards and

The first engagement for the Gladiators of No 3 Sqn RAAF took place on 19 November 1940 against a large formation of CR.42s, when these three pilots all made claims. On the left is Flg Off Alan Rawlinson, who claimed two damaged, whilst Flt Lt Pelly (in the centre) was credited with one destroyed. To the right is Flg Off Alan Boyd, whose three victories set him well on the way to becoming the RAAF's sole Gladiator ace (*J D R Rawlings collection*)

rejoined my escort (Flg Off A H Boyd). These three then broke off. During the battle, at approximately 1405hrs, I turned as two E/A were attacking me from the rear, and I got in one good burst. This aircraft issued black smoke, which increased in intensity until he finally broke away. I saw him flying away in a cloud of black smoke.'

It was a dramatic debut for No 3 Sqn's career in the fighter role, and for Boyd the start of what would eventually make him the sole RAAF Gladiator ace – Alan Rawlinson, too, later became an ace. Not to be outdone, the following day No 112 also had a very successful combat, during which it made its final claims in the desert. A reconnaissance near Sidi Barrani was attacked by 18 CR.42s, and whilst the Hurricane escort stayed with their charges, No 112 Sqn's six Gladiators dived on the Italians and quickly destroyed eight for no loss. Amongst the scorers were Acworth, who claimed his second victory and shared another, and Sgt 'Paddy' Donaldson, who claimed his first – he too went on to become a Gladiator ace with six victories.

On 1 December No 112 Sqn began ferrying Gladiators to the Royal Hellenic Air Force, and a month later moved to Amriya, from where it eventually moved to Greece. Further west, on the night of 7/8 December, the Allied counter offensive began, with No 3 Sqn in support.

The 10th proved to be a fruitful day for the Australians, who claimed an Ro.37 shot down in the morning. Later, a patrol was sent over the frontline, and 12 CR.42s were found strafing British positions. The Gladiators waded into the Fiats. In a brisk fight, three Italian fighters were destroyed without loss – one each to Sqn Ldr McLachlan, Flt Lt Gatward and Flt Lt Steege, who also claimed a probable (the first of his eventual total of eight victories). No 3 Sqn's next big fight came soon after midday on 12 December, when five Gladiators intercepted 17 CR.42s north of Sofari. Three Fiats were again destroyed without loss, including one to Boyd and another to future ace, Flg Off 'Woof' Arthur.

Often outnumbered, the aggressive Australians had so far achieved their successes for little loss, but that changed on the 13th. Six Gladiators on an early morning patrol attacked a formation of five S.79s attacking troops near Sollum, and a Savoia fell to Gordon Steege's fire. However, eight escorting CR.42s then intervened, and in the vicious fight that ensued, no

Alan Rawlinson was flying L9044/NW-Z during the epic 19 November clash, this aircraft having previously seen service with the Royal Egyptian Air Force (*Neil Mackenzie*)

Flg Off W S 'Woof' Arthur of No 3 Sqn claimed two CR.42 kills whilst flying Gladiators in December 1940. However, on 13 December his aircraft was badly damaged and he only bailed out with great difficulty. Arthur later served in New Guinea, and his total of eight victories included Italian, German and Japanese aircraft (*B Cull*)

Gladiator I K6142, which had previously been RT-U with No 112 Sqn and damaged in a take-off accident at Gerawla on 31 December 1940. At the controls was Flg Off John Jackson, who on 25 June 1941 downed a Vichy Potez 63 to become an ace. His final total was seven kills (*Neil Mackenzie*)

No 3 Sqn's final combat with the Gladiator took place over Mechili on 25 January 1941. Amongst the aircraft that engaged the Italians was L9044/NW-Z, flown by Flg Off Peter Turnbull, and which now sported the name *Sweet Sue* below the cockpit. Turnbull damaged a G.50 in the fight, which was included within his tally of 12 destroyed, 1 probable and 2 damaged. He was killed in New Guinea in 1942 whilst commanding a Kittyhawk unit (*Neil Mackenzie*)

less than five Gladiators fell to the enemy. Flg Off Winten bailed out, Gaden was killed and Boyd and Gatward crash-landed – the former's N5782 was repairable, and later got airborne with both Boyd and Gatward crammed into its tiny cockpit. Arthur's aircraft (N5752/ NW-G) was also severely damaged, and he too decided to bail out but became entangled, first with his oxygen tube and then with the wing bracing wires. Initially trapped, Arthur was finally thrown clear of the crashing Gladiator at around 1,000 ft, and he parachuted to safety. Following this reverse, No 3 Sqn stood down from operations until the 18th.

Support to the 6th Australian Division assault on Bardia continued, but No 3 Sqn only experienced one further combat during the latter part of December. On the 26th, eight Gladiators sighted a formation of S.79s escorted by six CR.42s, with a top cover of 18 more, over the Gulf of Sollum. Two went for the S.79s, forcing their withdrawal, and two of the Fiat fighters were shot down into the sea, another was probably destroyed and five others damaged for no loss. Claims included 'Woof' Arthur in N5753 with one shot down and three damaged, and Steege for a destroyed and a damaged. Another future 12-kill ace, Flg Off Peter Turnbull, opened his scoring with a probable. Soon afterwards Bardia fell, yielding the capture of 40,000 Italian prisoners and much war matèriel.

On 11 January 1941, No 3 Sqn's Lysander flight re-equipped with Gladiators, allowing the unit to at last concentrate on flying just the fighter type. The assault on Tobruk began on the 21st, and three days later a patrol over Mechili, comprising Sqn Ldr Campbell, Flt Lt Rawlinson, Flg Off Turnbull and Plt Off Campbell, encountered the monoplane Fiat G.50 for the first time. Five were spotted about 8,000 ft above them, and they immediately dived on the biplanes. Peter Turnbull, who was attacked several times, takes up the story:

'My position in the flight was astern of the vic formation. Each time I was attacked from astern and above, to avoid being hit I made a side-slipping turn back underneath. As the E/A passed overhead, it made a climbing turn to the left, and I was able to get well within range by turning right. I was attacked nine times, and each time I carried out the above action, but three of my guns ceased to fire owing to stoppages during the first attack, and the fourth after the fifth attack. I could see bullets hitting E/A during the third, fourth and fifth attacks, which were at close range.'

After the combat, Flg Off Campbell was posted missing and his CO namesake forced to land in the desert. The two surviving Gladiators also suffered damage. This was in fact the last time the Gloster fighter encountered the *Regia Aeronautica* in the hands of No 3 Sqn, for on 29 January the unit received its first Hurricane Is, becoming fully equipped on 8 February. The squadron went on to become one of the leading fighter units in the Mediterranean, the foundation for this success having been well laid by the Gladiators, which fought five actions resulting in the destruction of 12 Italian aircraft for the loss of five fighters and two pilots.

MALTA AND THE MEDITERRANEAN

More than any other action in which the Gladiator was involved, it was Malta which gave it undying fame. Fuelled by the need to prop up civilian morale, the myth of the three Gladiators 'Faith', 'Hope' and 'Charity' caught the public imagination, and remains to this day. In reality, the single-handed defence of Malta by the ad-hoc Fighter Flight lasted less than two weeks, for after 21 June 1940 Hurricanes had arrived from the carrier HMS *Argus*. Nonetheless, the Gladiator Flight, manned by volun-

teer pilots, did face the might of the *Regia Aeronautica* alone for a time, and gained a number of successes.

The previous April, 18 crated Sea Gladiators had been off-loaded at Hal Far from HMS *Glorious*, and the Royal Navy agreed to some being made available to the RAF, which had no fighters on the island. Volunteers from the resident pilots of No 3 Anti-Aircraft Co-operation

'Faith', 'Hope' and 'Charity' – undoubtedly the most famous of all Gladiators, even if the legend is possibly more myth than fact. These three Sea Gladiators of the Hal Far Fighter Flight, photographed in June 1940, are N5520 (which survives to this day), N5531 and N5519 (*J Pickering*)

Unit and the Air Officer Commanding's Personal Staff Officer, Flt Lt George Burges, began training with the Hal Far Fighter Flight, commanded by Sqn Ldr 'Jock' Martin. Thus, when hostilities broke out on 10 June, there was at least a trained fighter defence for Malta and its vital naval base.

The first Italian raid occurred the following day by several formations of S.79s, which were intercepted by the CO, George Burges and Flg Off 'Timber' Woods. The bombers easily outpaced the biplanes, as Burges later recalled. 'As soon as I opened up, the Italians poured on the coal and

The first confirmed victory over Malta was made on 22 June 1940 by Flt Lt George Burges, who is seen here sitting in the cockpit of the aircraft he used to score this kill, N5519/R. He shot down a C.200 the very next day, and went on to claim a further five victories, and be decorated with the first DFC awarded to a Malta fighter pilot (*NWMA*)

Sea Gladiator N5520 was used in the initial skirmishes over Malta on 11 and 12 June 1940, with Flg Off J L Waters at the controls. It was later fitted with a Mercury VIII engine and Hamilton propeller from a Blenheim in order to keep it serviceable (*NWMA*)

the Gladiator just couldn't catch up with them.' He did, however, slightly damage one, whilst Woods had a tussle with a Macchi C.200 fighter, which was also damaged. Later in the day two Gladiators scrambled, and Flg Off John Waters (in N5520) believed he shot an S.79 down. He attacked another the next day, and again claimed it destroyed, although in fact neither of the bombers was damaged. After a brief lull, further raids followed, but the Gladiators enjoyed little success mainly due to the speed of the bombers.

The Flight lost two of its precious fighters in crashes on the 21st, but the Navy hastily issued replacements. Success at last rewarded the Flight's efforts during the afternoon of 22 June, when a lone S.79 flying a reconnaissance sortie over Malta was intercepted by Burges and Woods. Climbing to 14,000 ft over Marsaxlokk Bay, they were surprised to discover that they for once enjoyed the advantage of height. Burges, who was flying N5519, takes up the story:

'"Timber" Woods and I were on the 1600 hrs to dusk watch when the alarm went off. We took off and climbed as hard as we could go, as was the custom. We did not attempt to maintain close formation because if one aircraft could climb faster than the other then the additional height gained might be an advantage. Ground Control (the solitary AMES radar site – author) as usual gave us the position and course of the enemy, which turned out to be a single S.79 presumably on a photographic sortie.

'It came right down the centre of the island from Gozo, and on this occasion we were 2000-3000 ft above it. "Timber" went in first, but I did not see any results. I managed to get right behind it and shot off the port engine. I was told this happened right over Sliema and Valetta, and caused quite a stir in the population. The aircraft caught fire and crashed into the sea off Kalafrana.'

The first confirmed kill for the Malta fighters was Savoia S.79 MM22068 from 216° *Squadriglia*. Both pilots escaped from the burning aircraft and were eventually picked up from the sea, but the rest of the crew perished. The next day Burges and Woods again scrambled against an incoming raid, escorted by C.200s of 88° *Squadriglia*. Burges, again in N5519, engaged the bombers without effect. The escort then intervened and he was soon in a tight turning fight off Sliema.

Although faster, the Macchi was less nimble than the Gladiator, thus enabling Burges to 'belt him up the backside as he went past'. Eventually, Sgt Magg Molinelli's Macchi caught fire and he bailed out into the sea, from where he became a PoW. Woods' aircraft was damaged in the combat, but he redressed the balance on 28 June when he was credited with an S.79, although this aircraft had in fact returned severely damaged.

HMS *Eagle*'s Fighter Flight was an ad hoc unit formed by Cdr Charles Keighly-Peach. All his combats were undertaken in this Sea Gladiator, N5517/6-A, which is seen here touching down on *Eagle*'s deck in July 1940 (*R C Sturtivant collection*)

Soon after the Hal Far Flight had formed, a naval equivalent came into being. The air group from the carrier HMS *Eagle* lacked any fighters, so four Sea Gladiators – N5512, N5513, N5517 and N5567 – were issued. On 16 June 1940 a Fighter Flight was formed, led by *Eagle*'s Commander (Flying), Cdr Charles Keighly-Peach, who trained several Swordfish pilots in fighter tactics. On the morning of 11 July the Mediterranean Fleet was located by an Italian flying boat, and air attacks soon developed. The Sea Gladiators made interceptions but failed to have any success.

However, in the afternoon, Keighly-Peach (known as 'K-P' in naval circles), in N5517/6-A, and Lt Keith in N5513 found a formation of five S.79s below them, and they dived vertically to engage. 'K-P' went for the leading Savoia, making three attacks in to about 50 yards. The bomber began to burn and drop back, before spinning into the sea. The Gladiator was damaged by return fire, and 'K-P' was wounded in the thigh – the fragment was not removed until 1976! Fire from the fleet forced Keith to abandon his attack, although he was credited with one damaged.

Further action ensued two days later against attacks by Aegean- and Libyan-based bombers when the fleet was south of Crete. *Eagle* launched the Sea Gladiators early, and at 0750 hrs Keighly-Peach spotted a lone S.79. Making three diving attacks from out of the sun, he reported the port wing on fire as it spun into the sea.

Three hours later, in company with Lt Keith, he sighted three Savoias approaching from the north-east. Keith fired at the left-hand aircraft, and was joined by his leader until the unfortunate bomber crashed into the sea. The sole survivor was picked up by HMS *Hereward*. In mid-afternoon, Kenneth Keith was launched against a formation of tri-motored bombers, believed to have been S.81s, from 200° *Squadriglia*, and after a beam attack and a stern chase he sent one down into the sea to end a very successful day for the Flight.

The *Eagle* Fighter Flight's next action in July came on the 29th, when another S.79 was brought down. Two days later, over Malta, 'Timber' Woods made the first Gladiator claim for a month when, in a stiff fight against up to nine CR.42s of 23° *Gruppo*, he brought down Capt Antonio Chiodi for the fourth of his 6¹/₂ kills. The fight was not one-sided,

This poor, but very rare, photograph is of the Royal Navy's leading Sea Gladiator pilot, Cdr Charles Keighly-Peach, who in five successful combats claimed 3¹/₂ destroyed; 1 probable and 1 damaged. A regular officer, he was awarded a DSO for his leadership of *Eagle*'s Fighter Flight, which provided much needed air defence for the fleet against the *Regia Aeronautica* (*B Cull*)

Another Sea Gladiator serving with HMS *Eagle's* Fighter Flight was N5567/6-C, which was flown by Lt A N Young on 17 August 1940 when he shared in the destruction of an S.79 off Bardia. It was also used by Lt R H Oliphant to probably destroy another S.79 on 13 October. The fighter later transferred to 805 NAS on Crete, where it was probably lost when the island fell to the Germans in May 1941 (*B Cull*)

All three of the Sea Gladiators attached to 806 NAS in October 1940 prepare for flight from the deck of HMS *Illustrious* once the launch of the more numerous Fulmars, visible in the background, has been completed. The nearest aircraft is N5549, whilst the fighter running up closer to the stern is N5513 (note that a third Sea Gladiator is parked behind the latter biplane fighter). Both were used to shoot down a Cant Z.501 on 8 November, N5513 being flown by Navy ace 'Jackie' Sewell (*D J Tribe*)

however, as Serg Manilo Tarantino shot down Flg Off Peter Hartley in N5519, the aircraft falling into the sea off Marsaxlokk Bay. Flg Off Jock Barber witnessed the action:

'Peter must have been hit in his centre tank, because his Gladiator burnt like a magnesium flare – a brilliant light in the sky. He actually bailed out after his aircraft caught fire, and he fell into the sea. He was very badly burnt, particularly about the knees, arms and face.'

This was the only Malta Gladiator to have been lost in air combat.

The end of July also saw the award of the DFC to Flt Lt Burges, and in early August the Fighter Flight was incorporated into the newly formed No 261 Sqn, which thus flew a mix of Hurricanes and Sea Gladiators – pilots regularly flew both types in combat, Burges for example claiming four of his seven kills on the Hurricane.

During the middle of August the fleet conducted a bombardment of the Libyan port of Bardia. On the 17th, as the ships sailed for Alexandria, they came under intense Italian air attack. *Eagle's* Sea Gladiators, meanwhile, had flown ashore to Sidi Barrani to provide cover for the fleet in conjunction with RAF Gladiators. Having become separated from his flight, 'K-P' attacked an S.79 over the naval vessels, seeing one man bail out before he lost it – he then attacked another without result. Meantime, Lts Keith and Young shared another Savoia with an aircraft from No 112 Sqn, whose pilots made further claims. Italian losses were indeed heavy, with four bombers being destroyed and eight damaged.

The following week the fleet sortied again, and off Crete on 31 August 'K-P', in N5517, launched with N5567, flown by Lt Olpihant, to intercept a shadower. They found a Cant Z.506B at 6000 ft, and the events that subsequently transpired were later being told by Keighly-Peach:

'I think the crew of the Cant must have been asleep, as I was offered no opposition, and I felt I was almost committing murder – it was too easy. The Cant ditched off the coast off Crete, and I saw the crew descending via parachutes, and they must have landed close enough to land to be able to swim ashore.'

This was 'K-P's final confirmed claim, making him the leading Fleet Air Arm Sea Gladiator pilot. His subsequent award of the DSO was well deserved.

Soon afterwards the new carrier HMS *Illustrious* arrived with a full compliment of Fulmars, and the pressure on *Eagle's* small fighter flight eased. Over Malta, meanwhile, sorties by No 261 Sqn's Gladiators continued to be flown by a number of pilots, some of whom

49

like Sgt Fred Robertson became aces on the Hurricane. Success eluded the biplanes until early November, when on the 2nd George Burges (flying N5520) scrambled with two others against an incoming raid with a strong fighter escort. In a dogfight against an estimated eight CR.42s, he claimed one shot down and another damaged. Back at sea, on 6 November two heavily escorted convoys sailed for Malta.

To support its fighter compliment against the expected opposition, *Illustrious* embarked at least three Sea Gladiators from 813 NAS, these being duly attached to 806 NAS. They drew first blood two days later when, at 1230 hrs, 806 NAS's Lt Roger Nichols in N5549 and Sub Lt Jack Sewell in N5513 destroyed a Cant Z.501 from 186° *Squadriglia*, flown by Ten Primatesta's crew. A contemporary naval account noted:

'It struck the water and two members of the crew of five were unable to extricate themselves – they were drowned. The other three, a Naval Sottotenente, a Sergente Maggiore and a wireless operator, managed to scramble into the Cant's dinghy.'

Sewell was a rising star in the Fleet Air Arm, this being his tenth combat, and his eventual total was at least 6, with 7 shared destroyed. Action continued over Malta, although Hurricanes were now the main defenders, and by early 1941 No 261 Sqn had just four Gladiators on strength.

With Malta and the Navy carriers proving an increasing thorn in the Axis' side, the Luftwaffe took a hand. On 10 January 1941, Ju 87 Stukas delivered a devastating attack on *Illustrious*, which then limped into Grand Harbour for emergency repairs. The remnants of 806 NAS disembarked to assist in the island's defence, and it was one of the unit's Sea Gladiators that made the type's final claim over the battered island.

On the 24th Jack Sewell was airborne on a met recce when he noticed tracer fire passing his wing. He spotted a Ju 88 diving towards Hal Far, and following the intruder, shot it down off the coast for his fifth kill. His victim was probably Unteroffizier Ulrich's L1+HM of 4./LG1.

Thereafter, the surviving Gladiators were concentrated in No 261 Sqn, and used mainly for meteorological recces, being flown by a number of the successful Malta aces such as Flt Lt James MacLachlan (16½ victories) and Flt Lt 'Porky' Jeffries of No 185 Sqn (4 and 2 shared destroyed). The last known use of the Malta Gladiators was a met recce by N5520 in January 1942. Like old soldiers, they never died, but just faded away.

N5549 (one of the three Sea Gladiators transferred to 806 NAS aboard the *Illustrious*) is seen after it was blown on its nose on 9 November 1940 following its recovery after chasing a fleet 'shadower'. The previous day, whilst being flown by Lt Nichols, it had helped shoot down a Cant Z.501 (*B Cull*)

The final Gladiator victory over Malta fell to Navy Fulmar ace, Lt A J 'Jackie' Sewell, who brought down a Ju 88 on 24 January 1941. He was later killed in an flying accident whilst CO of a Corsair squadron in September 1943 (*C F Shores*)

The distinction of claiming the RAF's final Gladiator victory fell to this aircraft, N5851, on 26 September 1941. Serving with No 6 Sqn at the time, it had been scrambled with a Sgt Walter at the controls when a *Regia Aeronautica* S.81 attacked Kufra Oasis, on the Egyptian border. Firing some 1400 rounds, Walter was duly credited with its destruction (*Gen Lonsdale*)

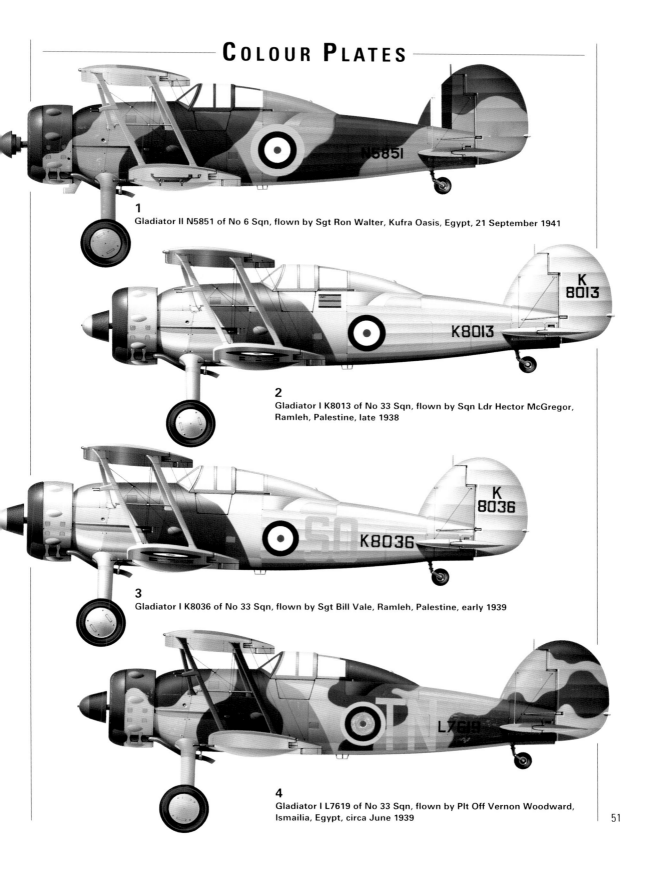

1
Gladiator II N5851 of No 6 Sqn, flown by Sgt Ron Walter, Kufra Oasis, Egypt, 21 September 1941

2
Gladiator I K8013 of No 33 Sqn, flown by Sqn Ldr Hector McGregor, Ramleh, Palestine, late 1938

3
Gladiator I K8036 of No 33 Sqn, flown by Sgt Bill Vale, Ramleh, Palestine, early 1939

4
Gladiator I L7619 of No 33 Sqn, flown by Plt Off Vernon Woodward, Ismailia, Egypt, circa June 1939

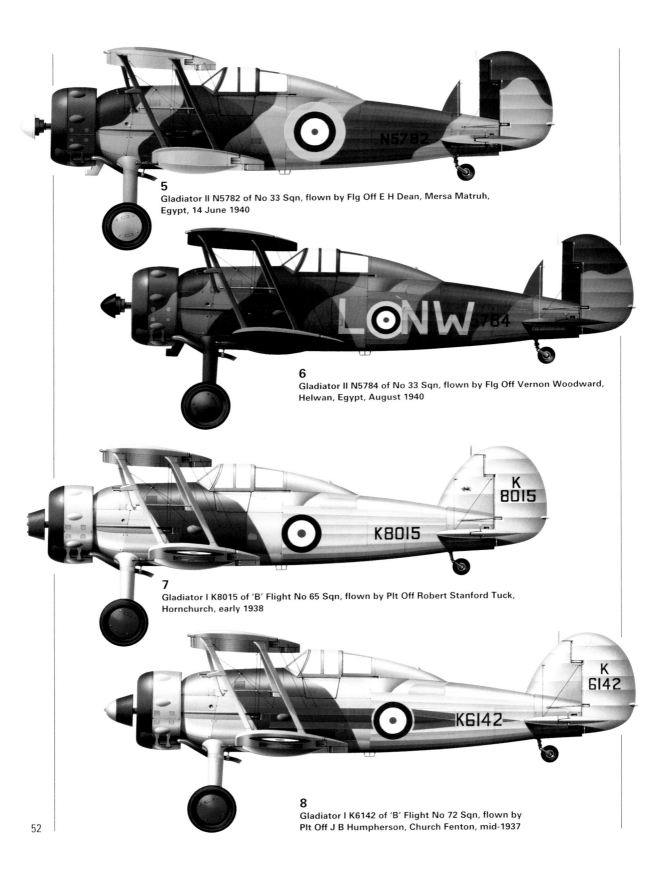

5
Gladiator II N5782 of No 33 Sqn, flown by Flg Off E H Dean, Mersa Matruh, Egypt, 14 June 1940

6
Gladiator II N5784 of No 33 Sqn, flown by Flg Off Vernon Woodward, Helwan, Egypt, August 1940

7
Gladiator I K8015 of 'B' Flight No 65 Sqn, flown by Plt Off Robert Stanford Tuck, Hornchurch, early 1938

8
Gladiator I K6142 of 'B' Flight No 72 Sqn, flown by Plt Off J B Humpherson, Church Fenton, mid-1937

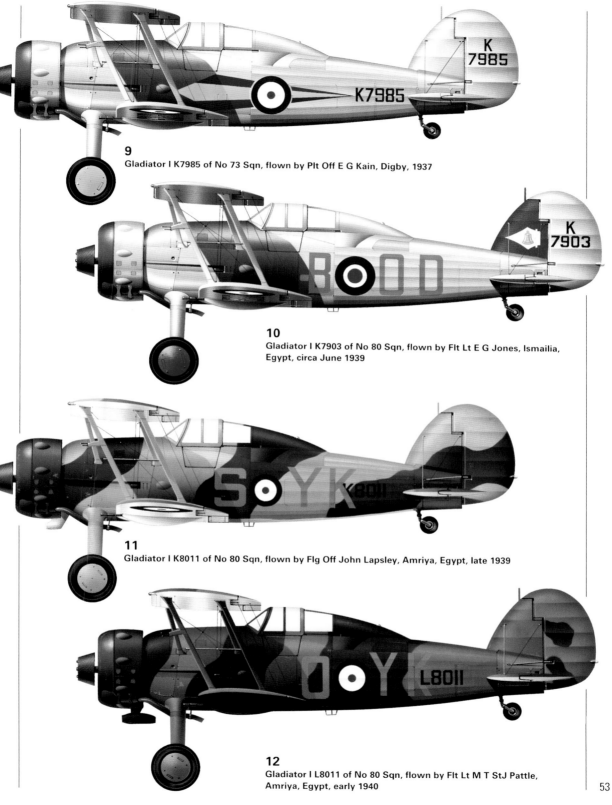

9
Gladiator I K7985 of No 73 Sqn, flown by Plt Off E G Kain, Digby, 1937

10
Gladiator I K7903 of No 80 Sqn, flown by Flt Lt E G Jones, Ismailia, Egypt, circa June 1939

11
Gladiator I K8011 of No 80 Sqn, flown by Flg Off John Lapsley, Amriya, Egypt, late 1939

12
Gladiator I L8011 of No 80 Sqn, flown by Flt Lt M T StJ Pattle, Amriya, Egypt, early 1940

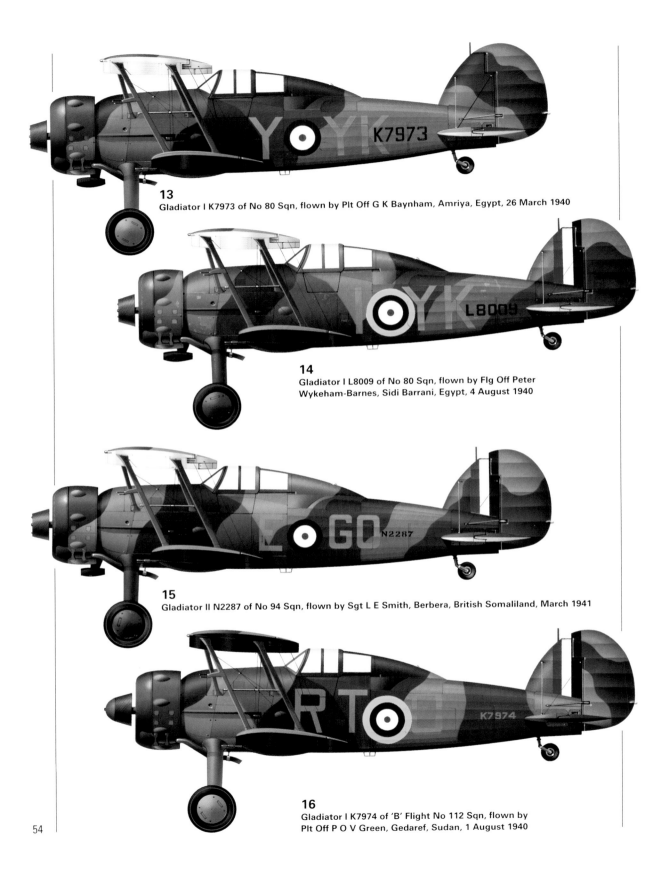

13
Gladiator I K7973 of No 80 Sqn, flown by Plt Off G K Baynham, Amriya, Egypt, 26 March 1940

14
Gladiator I L8009 of No 80 Sqn, flown by Flg Off Peter Wykeham-Barnes, Sidi Barrani, Egypt, 4 August 1940

15
Gladiator II N2287 of No 94 Sqn, flown by Sgt L E Smith, Berbera, British Somaliland, March 1941

16
Gladiator I K7974 of 'B' Flight No 112 Sqn, flown by Plt Off P O V Green, Gedaref, Sudan, 1 August 1940

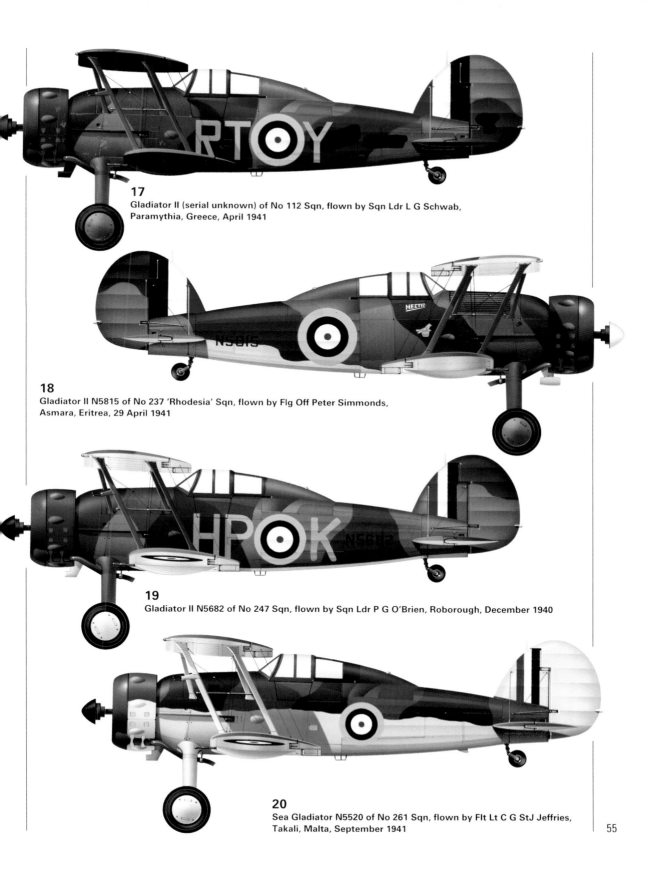

17
Gladiator II (serial unknown) of No 112 Sqn, flown by Sqn Ldr L G Schwab,
Paramythia, Greece, April 1941

18
Gladiator II N5815 of No 237 'Rhodesia' Sqn, flown by Flg Off Peter Simmonds,
Asmara, Eritrea, 29 April 1941

19
Gladiator II N5682 of No 247 Sqn, flown by Sqn Ldr P G O'Brien, Roborough, December 1940

20
Sea Gladiator N5520 of No 261 Sqn, flown by Flt Lt C G StJ Jeffries,
Takali, Malta, September 1941

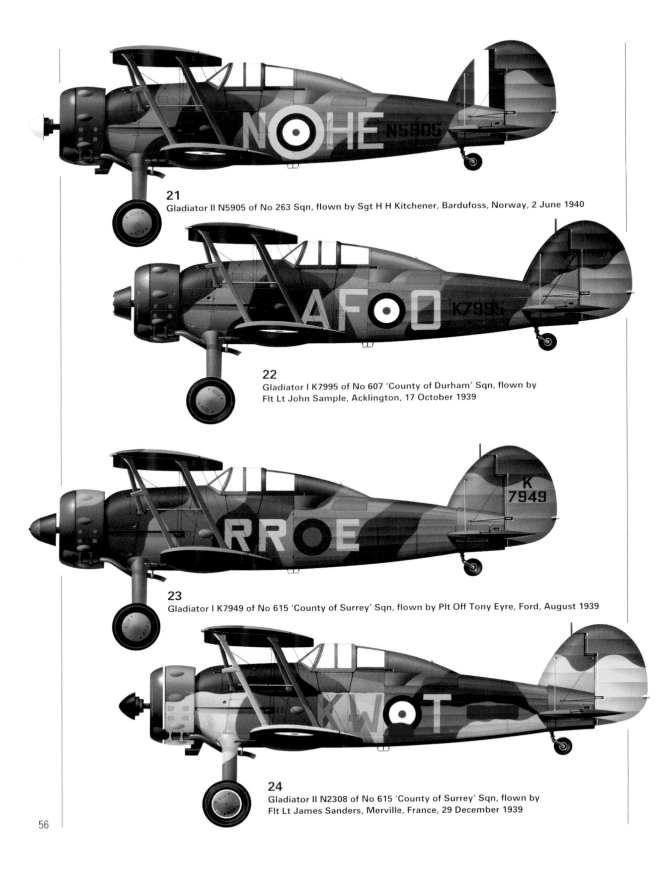

21
Gladiator II N5905 of No 263 Sqn, flown by Sgt H H Kitchener, Bardufoss, Norway, 2 June 1940

22
Gladiator I K7995 of No 607 'County of Durham' Sqn, flown by
Flt Lt John Sample, Acklington, 17 October 1939

23
Gladiator I K7949 of No 615 'County of Surrey' Sqn, flown by Plt Off Tony Eyre, Ford, August 1939

24
Gladiator II N2308 of No 615 'County of Surrey' Sqn, flown by
Flt Lt James Sanders, Merville, France, 29 December 1939

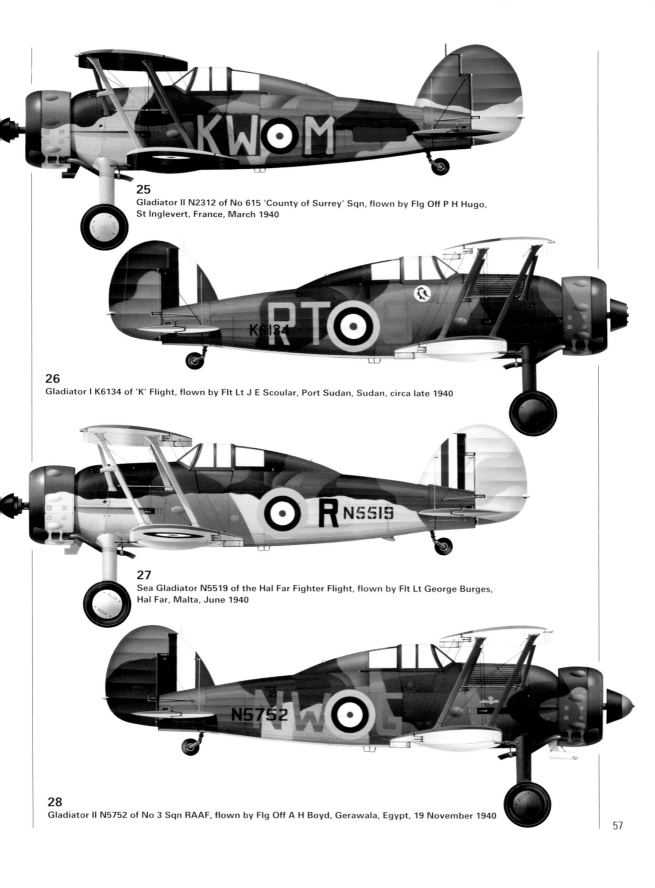

25
Gladiator II N2312 of No 615 'County of Surrey' Sqn, flown by Flg Off P H Hugo,
St Inglevert, France, March 1940

26
Gladiator I K6134 of 'K' Flight, flown by Flt Lt J E Scoular, Port Sudan, Sudan, circa late 1940

27
Sea Gladiator N5519 of the Hal Far Fighter Flight, flown by Flt Lt George Burges,
Hal Far, Malta, June 1940

28
Gladiator II N5752 of No 3 Sqn RAAF, flown by Flg Off A H Boyd, Gerawala, Egypt, 19 November 1940

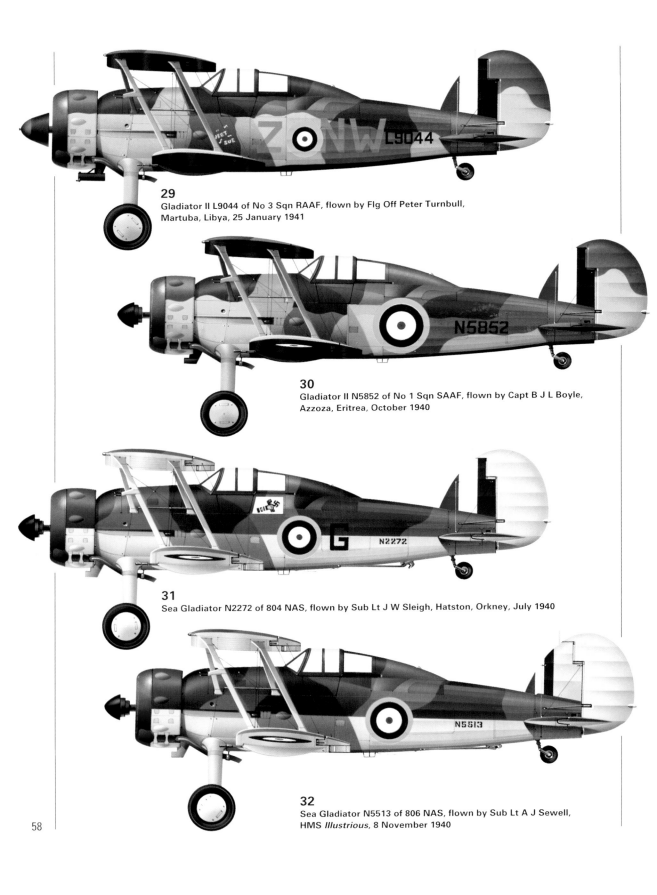

29
Gladiator II L9044 of No 3 Sqn RAAF, flown by Flg Off Peter Turnbull,
Martuba, Libya, 25 January 1941

30
Gladiator II N5852 of No 1 Sqn SAAF, flown by Capt B J L Boyle,
Azzoza, Eritrea, October 1940

31
Sea Gladiator N2272 of 804 NAS, flown by Sub Lt J W Sleigh, Hatston, Orkney, July 1940

32
Sea Gladiator N5513 of 806 NAS, flown by Sub Lt A J Sewell,
HMS *Illustrious*, 8 November 1940

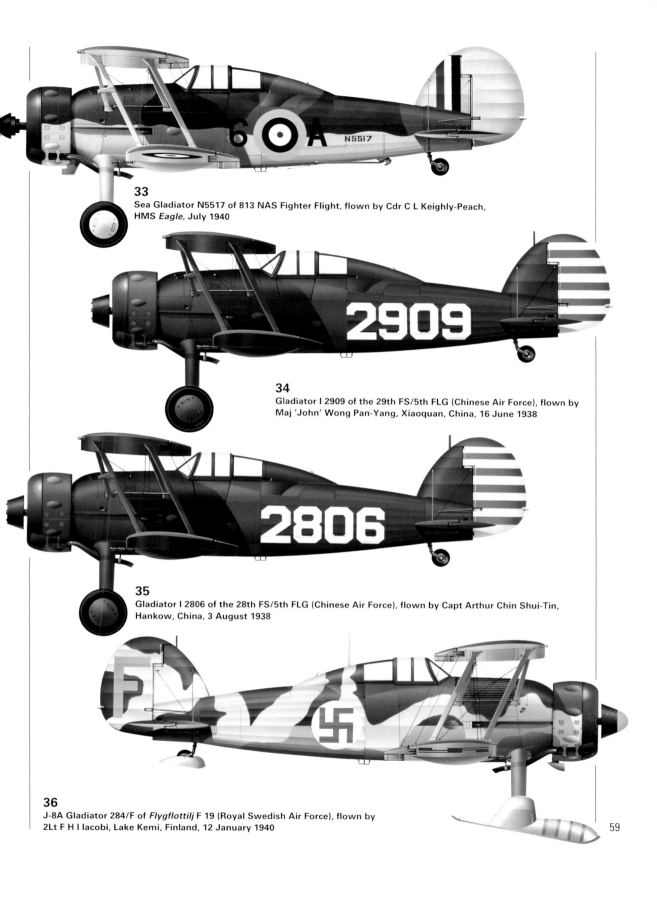

33
Sea Gladiator N5517 of 813 NAS Fighter Flight, flown by Cdr C L Keighly-Peach, HMS *Eagle*, July 1940

34
Gladiator I 2909 of the 29th FS/5th FLG (Chinese Air Force), flown by Maj 'John' Wong Pan-Yang, Xiaoquan, China, 16 June 1938

35
Gladiator I 2806 of the 28th FS/5th FLG (Chinese Air Force), flown by Capt Arthur Chin Shui-Tin, Hankow, China, 3 August 1938

36
J-8A Gladiator 284/F of *Flygflottilj* F 19 (Royal Swedish Air Force), flown by 2Lt F H I Iacobi, Lake Kemi, Finland, 12 January 1940

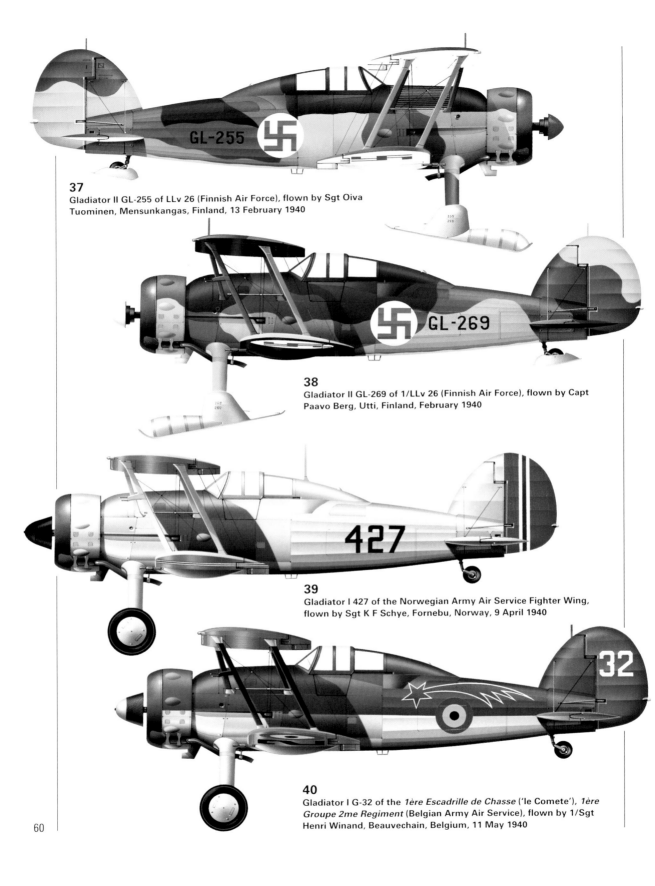

37
Gladiator II GL-255 of LLv 26 (Finnish Air Force), flown by Sgt Oiva Tuominen, Mensunkangas, Finland, 13 February 1940

38
Gladiator II GL-269 of 1/LLv 26 (Finnish Air Force), flown by Capt Paavo Berg, Utti, Finland, February 1940

39
Gladiator I 427 of the Norwegian Army Air Service Fighter Wing, flown by Sgt K F Schye, Fornebu, Norway, 9 April 1940

40
Gladiator I G-32 of the *1ère Escadrille de Chasse* ('le Comete'), *1ère Groupe 2me Regiment* (Belgian Army Air Service), flown by 1/Sgt Henri Winand, Beauvechain, Belgium, 11 May 1940

GREECE

At 0530 hrs on the morning of 28 October 1940, Italian forces invaded Greece from occupied Albania after a brief ultimatum had been turned down by the Greek government. The hard-pressed Greeks soon issued a request for help which, although desperately short of men and material in North Africa, Britain was obliged to honour. Amongst the forces allocated was the experienced No 80 Sqn, led by Sqn Ldr W J 'Bill' Hickey. By early November, 'new' replacement Gladiator IIs had been delivered to the unit in Egypt, and on the 17th 'Pat' Pattle's 'B' Flight flew to Eleusis, near Athens, via Crete. 'A' Flight soon followed.

On the 19th 'B' Flight moved north to Trikkala, in the centre of the country, and that afternoon, led by three Greek PZL P.24s, it flew a patrol of the Albanian border. Several Italian formations were seen, and Pattle, flying on the CO's wing, spotted some CR.42s. A rather colourful wartime report relates the start of the action:

'He broke formation and swung past the CO to attract attention (R/T silence had been briefed – author), waggling his wings furiously. Just in time, the Gladiators broke into the attacking Fiats as Pattle flick-rolled onto the tail of one of the Italians. The pilot put his nimble biplane "through the book" in an effort to shake off the Gladiator. Pattle clung to his opponent's tail like a limpet. In desperation the Italian went into a steep dive, violently side-slipping, but it was all in vain. A long burst and the CR.42 was a flaming pyre in a Greek field. The Gladiator had drawn first blood!'

In this fight over Koritza, the squadron claimed nine destroyed, including two by Plt Off 'Shorty' Graham. Sgt 'Cas' Casbolt also scored the first of his $13^1/_2$ victories in this combat, whilst Plt Off Bill Vale (flying N5766) downed one and shared another. After their initial attack, Pattle and his wingman, Plt Off 'Heimer' Stuckey, ended up alone at 15,000 ft. Spotting a fight to the north, they joined in and were engaged by five CR.42s and two G.50s in a head-on attack. A CR.42 pilot then pressed home his attack, and Pattle snap rolled over and ended up in a perfect firing position following some superb flying – a short burst into the cockpit area from 50 yards caused the Fiat to fall away in flames.

Meanwhile, Stuckey had shot-down another CR.42 and one of the G.50s – the latter was his fifth kill, elevating him to ace status. He had been wounded in the shoulder during the action, however, and he was evacuated to hospital after landing.

This sortie had proven to be a real success for No 80 Sqn, which had immediately established the same ascendancy over the *Regia*

The CO of No 80 Sqn for much of the Greek campaign was Sqn Ldr 'Tap' Jones (seen here flanked by his rigger and fitter), who took over following the loss of his predecessor, Sqn Ldr 'Bill' Hickey. All five of his victories were claimed in the Gladiator over Greece, and he duly received the DFC for these successes. A career officer, he later became Air Marshal Sir Edward Jones (*E G Jones*)

A clutch of No 112 Sqn pilots, including Flt Lt 'Algy' Schwab (in the sunglasses), chat between sorties outside the ops tent at Yannina in March 1941. Schwab took command of the unit the following month

Aeronautica in Greece as it had enjoyed in the desert.

Heavy rains subsequently water-logged Trikkala, and on the 26th a large detachment moved north to Yannina. The following day nine aircraft from Trikkala, led by the CO, patrolled the Yannina area. They encountered a number of S.79s, escorted by CR.42s, and in a brief fight two of the latter went down. One was claimed by flight commander Flt Lt 'Tap' Jones, in N5816, for the first of his five kills. The other successful pilot was Sgt Don Gregory, who (in N5776) had claimed the first of his eight Gladiator victories.

The next day six Gladiators, led by 'Tap' Jones, encountered a formation of ten CR.42s of 365° *Squadriglia* over Delvinakion. One immediately collided with a Gladiator, killing both pilots. In the ensuing battle, Jones drove several Fiats off the tails of his men, in the process shooting down two. He was himself then badly hit, with his instrument panel shattering in a welter of 12.7 mm bullets, and he was wounded in the neck. Don Gregory, who was again flying N5776, claimed three destroyed before escorting Jones back to base. In fact the Italians, who claimed four Gladiators, lost three Fiats, including that of five-kill ace Capitano Giorgio Graffer, who had already claimed four victories over Greece.

WINGS OF HELLAS

Success then came fast for No 80 Sqn, which was earning a well-deserved reputation. Pattle's next confirmed kill came during a morning weather check in N5832 near Argyrokastron on 2 December, when he destroyed an Ro.37 army co-operation biplane. A further patrol that afternoon saw him claim another, as did his wingman. The same day, 14 Gladiators were transferred to the hard-pressed Royal Hellenic Air Force (RHAF), whose 21 *Mira*, commanded by Capt Ionnis Kellas, was withdrawn to train on them. On 3 December No 80 Sqn concentrated at Larrissa, where it was reinforced by a detachment from No 112 Sqn led by Flt Lt C H Fry, who was destined to become an ace over Greece.

Early on 4 December 11 aircraft of No 80 Sqn, plus the detachment from No 112, returned to Yannina. That evening six of them, led by Pattle, escorted aircraft making supply drops to Greek troops in the mountains. Over Tepelene, in Albania, they encountered 20+ Italian fighters, and in the engagement which followed, a number of aces claimed kills.

Pattle downed a CR.42 into a hillside and set another on fire, from which the pilot bailed out, as did the pilot of a third he attacked. His aircraft received several hits in return. Casbolt and Bill Vale both claimed a CR.42 apiece, the latter recording in his logbook 'Offensive patrol Argyrokastron (1 CR.42)', thus taking his total to three and two shared kills.

The detachment returned to Larissa the following day, and over the next two weeks it rested and regrouped, with each of the veteran Gladiators being given a well-deserved overhaul.

Pre-war NCO pilot Ted Hewett scored three Gladiator victories within his eventual total of 16 kills. All his claims were made with No 80 Sqn over Greece (the rest being scored in Hurricanes), these victories earning him the DFM (*C F Shores*)

No 80 Sqn returned to operations on 19 December, and on the 20th two of the unit's greatest alumni – Pattle and Vale – were successful again. Pattle led a morning patrol over Tepelene which encountered a formation of S.79s, and he shot down Ten Berlinger's aircraft.

Two of the Gladiators then returned to base damaged, but the others continued on, spotting some S.81s, with an escort of G.50s. Pattle went for the middle aircraft of the leading element, hitting its centre engine, which caused the Savoia to come down north of Kelcyre. Vale was credited with a second bomber, although it actually staggered back to its Berat base with three dead crewmen aboard – the survivors just got clear of the bomber before it exploded. There was no interference from the escorting G.50s!

Even greater success came the next day during a mid-morning offensive patrol over Argyrokastron. Spotting enemy bombers, the three sections duly attacked, although this time the escorting CR.42s quickly intervened, and others led by Mag Oscar Molinari soon arrived. In spite of their greater numbers, the Italians employed poor tactics, with Pattle noticing that they would dive, fire at long range and then zoom back to altitude. Taking the initiative, his section followed their dive, and as they pulled up Pattle fired at one of the Fiats, which shed pieces of wing before crashing. Casbolt claimed another whilst Bill Vale was credited with no less than three in a superb display of gunnery.

Following the 25-minute combat, a total of eight CR.42s were claimed shot down against the loss of two RAF pilots, including the CO, Sqn Ldr Hickey. His loss was witnessed by Bill Vale:

'I saw him come out of a mass of '42s. His engine stopped and he jumped. The next moment one came in and fired at his parachute. I got that '42, and two others – one of them a 'flamer' – but by that time the CO's 'chute was blazing furiously. He didn't stand a chance.'

Sgt Don Gregory and Sid Linnard (who went on to attain ace status with No 274 Sqn in the desert) were both wounded. Gregory's combat report read in part:

'Turning round in a stall turn, I observed the leader of the '42s diving vertically, whilst the remaining two split, No 2 up and No 3 down. I had an advantage over the lower aircraft, and decided to attack it first.

One of the leading pilots of No 80 Sqn in Greece was Flg Off Bill Vale, who was also a pre-war regular sergeant pilot. Having already scored kills in North Africa, he became an ace in Greece during December 1940

Vale's regular aircraft (possibly N5784) bore the family coat-of-arms behind the cockpit access hatch

Yet another pre-war NCO pilot, Flt Sgt Don Gregory claimed eight victories on Gladiators over Greece, ranking him fourth amongst RAF pilots that flew the type. All his kills were CR.42s (*C F Shores*)

63

He attempted to come up under me. I had no difficulty in bringing my sight round to get a deflection shot, then turn astern of him. I followed him down. At the same time I observed the leading aircraft crash onto a hill and burst into flames.'

His two CR.42s took his score to seven, and resulted in a recommendation for the DFM. The CO's loss was a severe blow, and shortly afterwards 'Tap' Jones was appointed in his place.

Flg Off Nigel 'Ape' Cullen, described by a contemporary as 'a big, smiling, long-armed giant from Putney, with an irresistible offensive spirit and quite fearless,' claimed No 80 Sqn's final kill of the year the following day. Searching for intruders in the Athens area, he spotted a three-engined S.81 over the sea, which he brought down for his first confirmed victory. Bad weather then precluded much activity into the New Year, although amongst new arrivals was Malta ace Flt Lt 'Timber' Woods.

Flt Lt 'Timber' Woods (left) made his original claims over Malta with the Fighter Flight. At the start of 1941 he became a flight commander with No 80 Sqn, but was killed over Eleusis Bay on 20 April. Sitting to his left is Plt Off 'Shorty' Graham

The most successful Gladiator pilot with the Greek 21 *Mira* was its commander, Capt Ionnis Kellas, who is seen here on the right briefing his pilots. He escaped to Egypt, where he went on to command the first Greek Hurricane squadron formed within the RAF (*HAF Museum*)

Reinforcement for the meagre RAF fighter force came too, as in mid-January 1941 No 112 Sqn began moving across the Mediterranean. It was established at Eleusis towards the end of the month. By then No 80 Sqn had been in action for the first time in 1941, with 'Timber' Woods and 'Heimar' Stuckey sharing in the destruction of a Cant Z.1007 over Athens with a Blenheim from No 30 Sqn. The Gladiators had attacked from head-on and pressed into close range. Stuckey, flying K7902 in his first combat

since his wounding, was hit by return fire and broke away as his victim fell. He glided down towards the airfield at Hassani, but as he approached, horrified eye witnesses saw flames pour from the underside of his aircraft. The Gladiator was suddenly engulfed and it crashed into the ground, killing the unfortunate pilot. Stuckey was the only Commonwealth Gladiator ace to be killed in combat whilst flying the type.

At Yannina, Gladiator-equipped 21 *Mira*, led by Capt Ionnis Kellas, had also seen action in January, claiming the destruction of a Z.1007 over Salonika on the 25th – the successful pilot(s) remain unknown. No 80 Sqn's detachment at Athens rejoined the main body at Yannina a few days after this, and duly commenced a period of sustained and successful action.

During the afternoon of 28 January the new CO led a 15-aircraft patrol between Kelcyre and Premeti, where they encountered a group of four Fiat BR.20 and five Cant Z.5001 bombers. 'Ape' Cullen was credited with one of the latter, whilst Pattle, 'Cas' Casbolt and newly arrived Rhodesian Flg Off Eldon Trollip shared another. This share was Casbolt's fifth successful claim, thus giving No 80 Sqn yet another ace within its ranks. Heavy rain then restricted operations well into February, when better weather led to the resumption of fierce fighting.

No 80 Sqn's experienced hard core made further claims against the Italians when they next met on 9 February. At the time, the unit was flying in support of the Greek army as it pushed on to Tepelene. That same day Kellas led four Gladiators of 21 *Mira* (as well as some PZLs) over the Albanian border, where it encountered 18 S.79s of 104° *Gruppo* escorted by about a dozen G.50s and 12 CR.42s.

In a series of whirling fights, three of the Greek fighters, including the Gladiator flown by 1Lt Papaioannu, were hit by the Italian fighters. However, in return 2Lt Anastassios Bardivilias was credited with two fighters destroyed – he was shot down and killed in combat with G.50s the very next day. Two bombers were also claimed destroyed by Kellas, adding to the Z.1007 he had shot down whilst flying a P.24.

Later that same day, No 80 Sqn got airborne in four flights, and at around midday Pattle, who was leading, spotted some CR.42s off to port. Following clever use of cloud to mask his approach, he led his formation in to attack. Three of the enemy broke away, but two were trapped, Pattle going after the left-hand Fiat, which dived towards Tepelene.

His biography described the action as he 'followed closely behind the CR.42, firing short bursts every time the enemy appeared in his sights. Soon the Fiat was less than 20 ft above the trees, its pilot frantically manoeuvring to escape the stream of bullets which inched toward the cockpit. Above the houses of Tepelene "Pat" hung on grimly less than 50 yards behind and, as they shot over the outskirts of the town, got in a burst which ended the chase. The Fiat hit the ground at 200 mph and smashed itself into a thousand pieces.'

Whilst this fight went on at low level, further Italian fighters had appeared and many individual fights ensued. Flg Off Cullen despatched one Fiat with four well-aimed bursts, whilst Bill Vale and 'Cas' Casbolt also scored, as did Don Gregory, who claimed his eighth, and final, victory. Another future 'ace', Flg Off 'Jimmie' Kettlewell, scored his first kill – he ended the campaign with five and a probable.

Flt Lt 'Jimmie' Kettlewell had served with No 80 Sqn from 1938, and he claimed three victories flying Gladiators over Greece with the unit in February 1941. Switching to Hurricanes, he scored twice more before the end of the campaign. One of these was the Bf 110 that had just shot down No 33 Sqn's CO, Sqn Ldr 'Pat' Pattle (*E G Jones*)

A busy day continued with the first Italian raid on Yannina, although little damage was done. Just as the enemy aircraft left their target, the first seven Gladiators of No 112 Sqn arrived to support the hard-pressed pilots of No 80 Sqn. The day ended with the welcome news of the award – long overdue in the eyes of many – of the DFC to Flt Lt 'Pat' Pattle for, as the citation declared, 'In all engagements he has been absolutely fearless and undeterred by superior numbers of the enemy'.

The greatest Commonwealth ace of them all, Flt Lt 'Pat' Pattle is seen in the cockpit of his Gladiator in Greece – note his family crest. The South African's final total of claims will never be certain, but it is likely to be 'around' 50, making him the RAF's leading fighter pilot by some margin. He was also universally respected as both a pilot and leader in the air (*C F Shores*)

Following the Italian raid, aircraft were maintained at readiness to counter any further attacks. And on 10 February the first bombers appeared at mid-morning, and aircraft proceeded to strike the base at regular intervals throughout the day. Cullen attacked several raids over Yannina before sending an S.79 crashing into a lake with its engines on fire. Some attacks got through, and several bombers were damaged by the defenders, including two by 'Pat' Pattle – his last claims with the old biplane. His final tally with the Gladiator stood at $15^{1}/_{2}$ destroyed, $3^{1}/_{2}$ probables and 5 damaged, making him the most successful pilot with the type.

Further Italian attacks developed on the 11th and these enjoyed some success. Changes were in the air, however, for No 80 Sqn was to re-equip with Hurricane Is. The first were delivered to Paramythia exactly one week later.

No 112 Sqn, meanwhile, had begun to perform its share of patrols, and on the afternoon of 20 February the weather cleared sufficiently for a supply drop escort to be flown by nine of the unit's Gladiators, along with eight from No 80 Sqn. The Italians ran into the Gladiators north of Klysoura, where a sharp engagement took place. 'Ape' Cullen shot down a CR.42 and a G.50 to become an ace, although his aircraft was also damaged in his last combat in the Gladiator. He later wrote:

'The leader came into close range and then flicked over on its back and dived down. I did a half roll and got into position dead astern. Four long bursts and the enemy caught fire and crashed into a snow-covered hill. Then engaged another G.50 and got in some good deflection shots. Saw two formations of biplanes, which I thought were "Glads", and went to take a look at them. They were CR.42s. Got on the tail of one, gave him a burst, and he went down on his back, and the pilot bailed out. The others made off at once. Just as well – I hadn't any ammo left!'

Although this Gladiator II (N5829/RT-Z) clearly wears the markings of No 112 Sqn, its record card only reflects service with No 274 Sqn and No 1411 Flt. That it served in Greece is beyond doubt, for it was used by Flg Off Vale of No 80 Sqn to destroy a G.50 and an S.79 over Himari on 28 February 1941. This was the only time that Vale flew the aircraft, so he had probably borrowed it from No 112 Sqn (*author's collection*)

No 112 Sqn also opened its Greek 'book' during this action when Flt Lt 'Algy' Schwab sent a G.50 down in flames for his fifth victory. Persistent rain then affected air operations over the mountains for the next week. However, on 28 February it cleared, and in the afternoon a mixed formation of Hurricanes and Gladiators from No 80 Sqn were joined by No 112 Sqn for a patrol over the Greek offensive in the Tepelene area. Flying at 14,000 ft, the RAF fighters spotted an enemy formation of BR.20s and escorts below them. The Hurricanes performed the initial interception, but when a further formation of Italian fighters was spotted the biplanes also joined in the fray.

The Gladiator pilots took on the clutch of G.50s over Albania, with Bill Vale (in N5829) downing a Fiat fighter over Himari. He followed this up minutes later with an S.79 – these were his last claims with the Gladiator, as were the G.50 and CR.42 destroyed by 'Jimmie' Kettlewell. A few of the No 80 Sqn pilots still flying the Gloster fighter also claimed kills, including 'Tap' Jones, who destroyed two CR.42s to thus become an ace.

No 112 Sqn also became involved in the fight to the degree that all of its pilots made claims, including Flt Lt Joe Fraser. He attacked a CR.42, and to his horror he watched his opponent bail out and suffer a parachute failure. Fraser also downed a G.50 that flew into a mountainside.

Charles Fry, the Australian commander of 'B' Flight No 112 Sqn, made his first claims with a CR.42 and a G.50. He too had become an ace by the end of the campaign, but was captured in Crete in May after having just scored his fifth kill. 'Paddy' Donaldson got a G.50 (probably that flown by Ten Traini of 394° *Squadriglia*) and another future Gladiator ace, Canadian Flg Off Homer Cochrane, secured his first kill when he despatched a CR.42. This day had been a huge success for the RAF fighter force, in spite of the inevitable confusion and resultant over-claiming.

For No 80 Sqn it was indeed a grand way to finish with its Gladiators, before handing them over to No 112 and concentrating on operating Hurricanes. Two days later the award of DFCs to 'Tap' Jones and to 'Ape' Cullen was announced – like Pattle and Woods, the latter ace was to be lost in the maelstrom of the coming German *blitzkreig* on Greece.

BALKAN *BLITZKRIEG*

No 112 Sqn, as the sole RAF Gladiator unit in Greece, continued fighting alongside the Hurricanes of Nos 33 and No 80 Sqns. On 4 March, south-west of Himare off the Albanian coast, its Gladiators, along with three from 21 *Mira*, found a group of about 15 G.50s and CR.42s preparing to attack a Blenhiem formation. As the Gladiators waded in, some of the G.50s sought refuge in cloud, but Flt Lt Joe Fraser was attacked by one and gradually his individual dogfight became separated from the main fight. Descending to 2,000 ft, he 'managed to get some deflection shots at a range of 100 ft and the opponent's engine started to smoke'. His third victory was subsequently confirmed.

Three days later 'Algy' Schwab's 'A' Flight detached to Paramythia, and on the 9th the Italian spring offensive began around Tepelene. The squadron was airborne at 1400 hrs, heading for the Tepelene area where a large formation of G.50s and CR.42s, escorting BR.20s, had been sighted. Sqn Ldr H L I Brown led No 112 Sqn down from 14,000 ft, giving one G.50 a long burst and causing it to crash into a hillside. Fry saw the bombers jettison their loads as he attacked one, and noted that the CR.42s stayed high. He then went for a G.50, which dived away vertically to crash, whilst Flt Lt Fraser sent a BR.20 down. Amongst the other successful British pilots on this occasion were 'Paddy' Donaldson, with two CR.42s, and Flg Off Richard Acworth with a G.50 – he had 'made ace' a few days earlier flying a Hurricane whilst on loan to No 80 Sqn.

Acworth was to claim his seventh, and final, kill a couple of days later when he brought down a G.50 near Bousi. Also on that patrol were two new pilots, Plt Offs Neville Bowker and 'Gerry' Westenra, who each shot down a G.50. Both men would eventually run their scores into double figures as the war progressed. However, No 112 Sqn's most successful day against what the squadron diary described as 'Mussolini's bedraggled eagles' came on 13 March. In mid-afternoon, the CO was leading 14 Gladiators north east of Tepelene at 17,000 ft when he radioed 'Tally Ho!'. A formation of homebound S.79s had been spotted with their escort. No 112 Sqn, along with some Hurricanes, dived on the fighters – identified as 'G.50s' (but probably C.200s) and CR.42s.

For Joe Fraser and Homer Cochrane, it proved to be a red letter day. Fraser attacked a CR.42 unseen, which burst into flames and fell near Bousi, and then went after another which 'Flick-rolled and dived away, but was followed down and hit with two long bursts, after which it levelled off and lost speed, with the pilot slumped in the cockpit. The aircraft then dived vertically into the ground north of Corovode.' Climbing back to 8,000 ft, Fraser then got onto the tail of another Fiat, which he fired at continuously until it burst into flames and crashed. Cochrane also destroyed three CR.42s to become an ace, whilst Plt Off Jack Groves took his score to four plus one shared when he claimed two more Fiat biplanes.

No 112 Sqn's 12 Gladiators met with about 40 enemy fighters late the following morning (14 March), but the CO had his tail shot off and only bailed out with difficulty. Charles Fry led his section into some BR.20s, and he duly shot one down near Kelcyre for his final Gladiator claim.

Meanwhile, Joe Fraser's section was jumped from above, and he was confronted by a G.50 making a head-on attack. Fraser managed to yaw, and thus evade the attack, and get in a short burst, after which the Fiat rolled onto its back and the pilot bailed out. It was his ninth, and final, kill, making him the RAF's third highest scorer with the Gladiator. Two more G.50s fell to Sgt 'Paddy' Donaldson, who thus too became an ace.

The Italians attacked No 112 Sqn's base on 26 March, with the first raid appearing at 0650 hrs. Schwab led off a section, but they returned without success. At 1250 hrs the enemy came back, as the unit records reveal:

'Flt Lt Schwab, Plt Offs McDonald, Bowker and Brunton were just off the ground when ten G.50s and/or Macchi 200s dived onto the aerodrome from the south. The first three got past, but the Glads got the following two sections and broke them up and put them off their objective – the aerodrome. A dogfight developed north-west of the aerodrome, and drifted over to the coast. One G.50 (actually a C.200 of 153° *Gruppo* – author) is believed to have been shot down by Flt Lt Schwab, but not confirmed as yet. One Gladiator was set on fire and burnt out on the ground. Plt Off Bowker's aircraft was badly shot up during the engagement, and he carried out a very well executed forced landing on the aerodrome.'

A Gladiator of No 112 Sqn burns on the airfield at Paramythia on 26 March 1941 after an effective strafe by C.200s of 153° *Gruppo*. Amongst those that took off to oppose them was Flt Lt 'Algy' Schwab, who claimed one probably destroyed (*E Bevington-Smith*)

Re-equipment was now in the offing, and although some pilots moved to Egypt, operations continued from Paramythia. Soon afterwards, on 3 April, the CO left, being replaced by 'Algy' Schwab. Two days later the situation changed dramatically with the German assault on Yugoslavia and Greece. At a stroke the RAF's hard won ascendancy was lost, and the Gladiators were instantly outclassed by the Luftwaffe's Bf 109s and Bf 110s. By the 8th the enemy had penetrated into Thrace and Salonika, and No 112 Sqn assisted in covering the withdrawal.

Five days later Commonwealth troops fell back on Thermopylae, and the unit was ordered to keep fighters over the area throughout the day. During one patrol Schwab shot down a G.50 for his final kill, and No 112 Sqn's last on the mainland. That evening the unit escorted the Yugoslav S.79 that carried King Peter and his Prime Minister as they fled into exile. The enemy advance forced an evacuation, initially south to Agrinon and then to the Athens area. In spite of enemy attacks, No 112 Sqn's Gladiators were kept on the ground, for they were no match for the marauding Messerschmitts. Finally, on 22 April, the unit was ordered to Heraklion, on the island of Crete.

The remaining Greek Gladiators had continued to fight on, however, and on the 15th Capt Kellas had been hit by a Bf 109 and crash-landed his burning aircraft. By the end of that day the RHAF had virtually ceased to exist, although Kellas survived to serve as commander of No 335 'Greek' Sqn, which was formed in North Africa in October 1941.

During the last week of April No 112 Sqn evacuated in good order with about a dozen aircraft, although few records survive from Crete. On 5 May Plt Off Westenra damaged a Ju 88, followed by a Bf 110 eight days later, although during the latter fight his Gladiator was badly damaged. On the 14th Plt Off Bowker destroyed a Bf 110 over Heraklion, as did Westenra, who shot down the Bf 110 flown by 14-victory *Experte* Oberleutnant Sophus Bagoe of II./ZG 26.

The German airborne invasion began a few days later under almost complete air superiority, and so the remnants of No 112 Sqn evacuated to Egypt to be re-equipped with Tomahawks.

ADEN, EAST AFRICA AND IRAQ

The Italian colonies in East Africa threatened British interests in the area following Benito Mussolini's declaration of war on the Allies in June 1940. To the south of Italian-occupied Ethiopia lay Kenya and British Somaliland, to the north the Sudan and across the Red Sea lay the vital port of Aden. Based at Sheik Othman was Sqn Ldr Freddie Wightman's No 94 Sqn, which was tasked with the day and night defence of the colony. The unit possessed eight Gladiator IIs in frontline service, with a further eight Mk Is in reserve.

The responsibility for Kenya's defence lay with the South African Air Force (SAAF), which had moved most of its squadrons into the colony during early 1940. Also mobilised and sent north was the sole Southern Rhodesian Air Force unit, which soon became No 237 'Rhodesia' Sqn RAF.

The SAAF's solitary fighter unit, No 1 Sqn, was equipped with a mix of Hawker Furies and Hurricanes, but in May 1940 pilots from 'C' Flight were flown to Egypt to train on Gladiators, 12 of which had been set aside for them.

Finally, with it appearing ever more likely that hostilities would erupt with the Italians, 'B' Flight of No 112 Sqn was sent to Summit, in the Sudan (with a detachment maintained at Port Sudan), in early June 1940.

Like the RAF, Italian bombers were immediately active following the declaration of war on 10 June, with raids by S.81s being flown against Port Sudan and Aden. On the night of the 13th, during the third raid against Aden, No 94 Sqn scrambled four Gladiators, one of which (N5590) was flown by Flg Off Gordon Haywood. Patrolling off Ras Imran Island, he shot down an S.81 from Diredawa-based 4° *Gruppo*, which was flown by SottoTen Paolelli. In a letter written home, Haywood later recalled:

'I caught one of the S.81s and made just one attack. I had taken off at 0440, and my attack was made well into dawn. The bomber caught fire and I recall flames ribboning in every direction. By now the other enemy aircraft were well away, and so I landed to re-arm and refuel – I was only airborne 30 minutes. The surviving crew from the bomber were later entertained in the Officers' Mess.'

No 94 Sqn produced no aces with the Gladiator, and its most successful pilot was its CO, Sqn Ldr (later Wg Cdr) Freddie Wightman. He achieved three victories, one over Assab, one over Aden and finally an Iraqi-marked CR.42 near Rashid during the Iraqi Revolt (*Ian Simpson*)

Flt Lt Eric Spence's Gladiator of No 237 'Rhodesia' Sqn was decorated both with the name *HECTIC* and a representation of the stone Zimbabwe bird, which became the emblem of the post-independence air force of Zimbabwe in 1980 (*E Spence*)

Camouflaged, and wearing unit code letters and toned down roundels, Gladiator II N2288/GO-A sits at Sheik Othman in 1940. It was one of four No 94 Sqn fighters involved in the first successful defence of Aden, on the night of 13 June, against Italian bombers (*I Simpson*)

Three hours later S.79s arrived overhead, and these were also intercepted by Gladiators from No 94 Sqn, which damaged two to cap a promising start for the squadron. Raids on Aden and Sudanese towns also continued, and No 112 Sqn's detachment drove off a raid on Summit on the 16th. Two days after this, Haywood spotted the Italian submarine *Galileo Galilei* off Aden. Summoning assistance, he led in other air and naval units, resulting in its capture – an unusual scalp for a fighter squadron!

Towards the end on the month No 94 Sqn was ordered to begin attacks across the Red Sea, the first of which was mounted on 28 June. The following day No 112 Sqn's Sudan detachment claimed its first kill when Plt Off Hamlyn scrambled in L7619 and found an S.81 of 28° *Gruppo*'s 10° *Squadriglia* flown by Capt Barone, the unit's CO. No 112's diary relates the event:

'Plt Off Hamlyn sighted 1 S.81 3000 ft above him, approaching from the south. He climbed up and delivered a quarter attack, developing into a stern chase. When attacked, the E/A dived and turned to the right, and at 4500 ft, after approximately 1000 rounds had been fired, it exploded and fell into the sea. Two men, presumed to be part of the crew were later picked up from a coral reef near the coast. This was the Detachment's first decisive combat, and proved that the Gladiator is more than a match for the S.81. Plt Off Hamlyn was approximately 30 yards behind the E/A when it exploded, and pieces of the structure damaged his windscreen, airscrew and ring & bead sight, while one large piece of petrol piping lodged in his engine.'

Further south, during an attack on Assab by No 94 Sqn on 2 July, Wightman and Sgt Dunwoodie bagged their first victories. Part of the CO's report read:

'I saw two CR.42s quite close to me at 1500 ft, circling to gain height. I flew towards them, and at the same time they both saw me and turned towards me. I closed with the leading one, and after a few seconds' manoeuvring, I succeeded in turning inside it and fired two long bursts at the cockpit, which immediately became a mass of flames and the aircraft

71

On 8 August 1940 the detachment of Gladiators from No 94 Sqn at Berbera, in British Somaliland, was caught on the ground by strafing CR.42s led by Capt Corrado Ricci. One of the aircraft destroyed was N5890, which had previously served with the Royal Egyptian Air Force (*No 94 Sqn Records*)

The second Italian to fall to No 112 Sqn's detachment in the Sudan was shot down near Gedaref on 1 August by Plt Off P O V Green, flying this Gladiator I (K7974/RT-O). It later served with the independent 'K' Flight (*A J Thorne*)

'C' Flight of No 1 Sqn SAAF arrived with its Gladiators in Kenya on 24 July 1940, and proved a useful reinforcement. The air raid warning system in use in-theatre was, however, primitive as illustrated by the air raid lookout in the tree! (*SAAF*)

at once fell nose first to the ground, blazing fiercely. It crashed just east of the Assab road about 1¹/₂ to 2 miles from the camp gates.'

The other CR.42 that latched onto Flt Lt Reid and was engaged by Bill Dunwoodie, who recorded:

'Enemy aircraft appeared and got on my tail. After a few minutes manoeuvring, I was able to get into a good attacking position and fired my guns. E/A's engine stopped and pilot started to glide. I attacked again, and as the E/A's wheels touched the ground it went over, first on one wing and then the other.'

With the *Regia Aeronautica* active in the south, at the end of July the Gladiators of 'C' Flight No 1 Sqn SAAF left Egypt for Kenya – nine more remained in the Sudan. Concern for the defence of British Somaliland led to a detachment of No 94 Sqn moving to Berbera, where it remained until the

The first claim by a SAAF Gladiator was made on 14 August 1940 when a Caproni Ca.133, attacking Wajir in Kenya, was damaged by Lt Colenbrander of No 1 Sqn. Here, he relates the action to his groundcrew whilst sheltering under an umbrella! He later served with No 2 Sqn in the desert, with whom he claimed two Ju 87s probably destroyed (*SAAF*)

evacuation, losing several aircraft to Italian strafing. In the north, No 112 Sqn remained vigilant, and on 1 August claimed another Italian, as the diary relates:

'0830 – Report arrived saying than an Italian Ca.133 was flying in the vicinity of Gedaref. Flight of three aircraft started up (K7086, flown by Flg Off Whittington, K7619, flown by Plt Off Chapman and K7974, flown by Plt Off Green – author), and Plt Off Green was first into the air, spotting the E/A almost immediately after taking off, when it was about 500 ft above him. After chasing the machine for about 50 miles, and delivering about 12 No 1 attacks, Green observed a member of the crew leave the aircraft by parachute. At the same time the starboard engine started smoking, and the machine force-landed in a clearing.'

On the 20th this detachment became 'K' Flight, by which time the South African Gladiators had seen action. Three Caproni Ca.133s attacked Wajir on 14 August, and they were met by Lt Colenbrander, who damaged one, wounding four of the crew. No 1 Sqn's first confirmed success came on 1 September, when a Sudan detachment patrol over Kassala was challenged by two CR.42s – these were duly shot down by Maj van Schalkwyk and Lt Coetzer.

Air defence remained a prime task for the Gladiator units, although the biplane's lack of speed compared with the S.79 proved a handicap. Strafing attacks on enemy airfields, however, proved fruitful, taking a steady toll of Italian aircraft. At the end of September No 1 Sqn's Kenya element, which included nine Gladiators, became No 2 Sqn, leaving No 1 in the Sudan. Based at Azzoza, No 1 Sqn's Gladiator detachment received a warning on 4 October, and three fighters took off. Flying over Metemma, the pilots spotted three CR.42s in line astern. In the dogfight that subsequently took place, Lt Viljoen downed one Fiat in flames. Capt Boyle's aircraft (N5852) was hit, but he continued his attack nonetheless, seeing the Fiat dive away out of control. This was 'Piggy' Boyle's first victory – he became an ace in early 1941.

This 'K' Flight pilot seen resting on the wheel of his Gladiator has not been positively identified, although he may be Plt Off Wolsey, who on 15 November 1940 intercepted two S.79s, which he damaged. Upon returning to base, he complained that he could not achieve more positive results due to his biplane's lack of speed (*C F Shores*)

73

FIRST ALLIED OFFENSIVE OF THE WAR

Later in October, No 2 Sqn in Kenya returned its Gladiators to No 1 Sqn, and on 1 November Lt Andrew Duncan (another future SAAF ace) claimed the first of his 5 1/2 kills. Escorting bomb-carrying Gauntlets, he spotted a number of Ca.133s attacking British forces around Gallabat. Approaching unseen from beneath, he attacked one of them from astern, followed by a pass from the beam. The Ca.133 slowly dived away and crashed.

Preparations for the British offensive continued, with the fighters giving cover from Italian aircraft. On 4 November an engagement took place with CR.42s of 412° *Squadriglia*, and Lt Theron's victim bailed out. 'Piggy' Boyle claimed a second Fiat. The following day Boyle took a detachment to 'Heston' strip, with 'K' Flight detached into Azzoza in support.

The first British offensive of the war began at dawn on 6 November, and led to some heavy air fighting. The first brush with enemy fighters came over Metemma at 0615 hrs, when three Gladiators of 'K' Flight were bounced by around eight CR.42s. All the British machines were shot down.

Soon afterwards, No 1 Sqn's CO, Maj van Schwalkwyk, was also attacked in the area en route to 'Heston'. His plight was phoned through by the 10th Indian Brigade HQ to 'Heston', from where in spite of the mud Boyle took off. He saw his CO's Gladiator burst into flames and a burning figure drop from it. Boyle was then fighting for his own life, as he later recalled:

'Bullets went over my shoulder into the dashboard. Oil came all over me. I was wounded by fragments of explosive bullets and the cockpit was full of smoke. I tried

The most successful SAAF Gladiator pilot was Capt 'Piggy' Boyle, who claimed two of his three victories in this aircraft, N5852. Photographed standing in front of it at 'Heston' LG on 5 November 1940, Boyle took off in the fighter the following morning in a brave, but vain, attempt to save his CO. Boyle was wounded in the action, and crash-landed. He was later decorated for his selfless bravery (*SAAF*)

Gladiator I K7977 has a well-worn appearance as it is prepared for flight in the Sudan sometime in 1940. Initially serving with 'B' Flight No 112 Sqn, the veteran fighter joined 'K' Flight upon its formation. On 6 November, during the offensive against Gallabat, the Gladiator was shot down in flames by a CR.42 and its pilot, Flg Off Haywood, killed (*E L Cooper*)

These two Gladiators were among those used for a short time by No 2 Sqn SAAF in Kenya, before they were passed back to No 1 Sqn. The aircraft furthest from the camera is N5815, which was later transferred to No 237 'Rhodesia' Sqn. Whilst serving with the latter unit, it was used by the squadron's leading pilot, Flg Off Peter Simmonds, to mount two successful strafing attacks on Italian airfields on 29 and 30 April 1941 (*O G Davies*)

to shake them off and bail out, but they continued to fire, so I crash-landed between the lines.'

He was quickly rescued and transported to hospital by an Indian Army officer, Maj J N Chaudhuri, who later became Indian Army Chief of the General Staff. For his very gallant action, Boyle received a well-earned DFC – sadly, the CO died from his burns the next day.

The situation was bad for the British, who had suffered severe fighter losses, as well as heavy bombing attacks by Ca.133s. A later patrol by 'K' Flt and No 1 Sqn spotted five bombers beneath them at 5,000 ft, but before they could attack they were hit by the escorting CR.42s, and Flg Off Haywood of 'K' Flight (no relation to the No 94 Sqn pilot) went down in flames. The SAAF aircraft broke into pairs, with Lts Coetzer and Pare tackling the fighters, each claiming one – this kill was not included in Robin Pare's eventual total of five destroyed, however. Duncan attacked a Caproni, which crashed on the road to Gondar for his second victory, whilst Lt John Hewitson began his route to 'acedom' when the Ca.133 he attacked fell out of control and crashed.

At the end of a day of bitter fighting Gallabat Fort had been captured from the Italians, although the loss of air superiority led to its evacuation the very next day. Early on 7 November the SAAF's Gladiators were active again, fighting CR.42s – one of these was credited to Lt Pare for his first confirmed claim. Several days later the surviving Gladiators of No 1 Sqn and 'K' Flight returned to Khartoum and Port Sudan, the former receiving further aircraft from No 2 Sqn.

The Italians continued to mount occasional raids on Aden and Port Sudan as 1940 drew to a close, and during the attack on 20 November No 94 Sqn achieved its final success of the campaign. At 0415 hrs Sqn Ldr Wightman (in N5627) met an S.81, as his report relates:

'Took off on the alarm and throttled back on patrol at 15,000 ft. I saw the bomber held in searchlights. I dived at full throttle, E/A opened fire at very long range, and when on the same level and dead astern of it I opened fire at about 300 yards, and as I closed I fired several long bursts aimed at a point where the port wing joined the fuselage. The incendiary appeared

Aces High! The leading pilots of No 1 Sqn SAAF pose for an unusual photo during March 1941. They are, from left to right, Capt Andrew Duncan DFC (5$\frac{1}{2}$ kills, with 2 in Gladiators), Capt Ken Driver (10, all in Hurricanes), Lt Robin Pare (5, with one in Gladiators), Maj Laurie Wilmot (4$\frac{1}{2}$, but none in Gladiators) and Capt 'Piggy' Boyle DFC (5$\frac{1}{2}$, including 3 in Gladiators) (*C F Shores*)

to be going into the E/A. I turned quickly to resume the attack and saw the E/A was doing a diving turn. I did a quarter attack from the port side, aiming at the front cockpit, and the attack developed into one from astern, slightly above. I dived again and fired a few more rounds. The E/A was then in a steep dive, and later there appeared to be flames coming from it. It crashed in the sea three miles east of Khormaksar.'

In correspondence written before he died, Wg Cdr Wightman added:

'I visited the hospital where the pilot of the S.81 was recovering from his ordeal. He was the Diredawa base commander, Colonello Via, who seemed keen to meet me, and showed no sign of resentment.'

At this time Hurricanes began arriving for No 1 Sqn, as did a new CO, Maj Laurie Wilmot, who went on to become a renowned ace and wing leader in the desert and Italy. In spite of severe supply shortages, Italian fighters remained a viable threat into 1941, shooting down a Gladiator and a Hardy on 12 January for example.

In preparation for a new offensive, No 1 Sqn was concentrated at a strip west of Kassala, from where it moved to Tessenei – the first airfield 'liberated' in Eritrea – on 23 January. There was further fighting on subsequent days, and on 3 February six of No 1 Sqn's Gladiators flew to a new strip at 'Pretoria'.

From there an attack on the Gondar area was opposed by CR.42s, and a big dogfight ensued in which Capts Le Mesurier and Boyle each shot a fighter down. Boyle later recalled:

Flt Lt John Scoular was already a very successful fighter pilot when he joined 'K' Flight in late 1940. His only victory with the Gladiator was an S.79 he brought down on 24 February 1941. He formed No 250 Sqn, equipped with Tomahawks, soon after scoring this kill, and used the Curtiss fighter to boost his final tally to 15$\frac{1}{2}$ kills (*J D R Rawlings collection*)

'I diced with one – he hit me and burst a tyre, but eventually I got so close I could see the badges of rank on his shoulder. He was flying in his shirtsleeves. He stood up and tried to get out but couldn't. I watched him fall, trailing smoke.'

This was Boyle's final Gladiator claim, although he attained ace status ten days later whilst flying a Hurricane – he was the leading SAAF Gladiator pilot in East Africa.

The only Gladiator victory for the Rhodesian-manned No 237 Sqn was achieved by Flg Off Peter Simmonds (the taller of the pilots seen here with a Gladiator at Umritsar, in Eritrea) when he brought down a CR.42 on 16 March 1941 (*Rodney Simmonds*)

RHODESIAN CLAIMS

'K' Flight, meanwhile, also remained active, receiving a formidable new CO when Flt Lt J E Scoular DFC took over on 13 February. A veteran of the Battles of France and Britain, he already had a dozen confirmed victories to his name. Scoular increased this tally during an early-morning patrol on 22 February, when he escorted some Blenheims en route to Massawa. In that area he found a lone S.79, which he shot down. During the remainder of the month No 1 Sqn mainly used the Hurricanes, and at the end of February the well-worn Gladiators were passed on to Flt Lt Eric Smith's 'B' Flight of No 237 Sqn.

The Rhodesian-manned squadron was then flying a mix of Hardys and Lysanders in the army co-operation role, for which the Gladiators would also be used. Operations began on 7 March in preparation for the assault on the Italian stronghold at Keren – the decisive battle of the Eritrean campaign, which opened on the 15th. Eric Smith later recounted:

'We had a frustrating time during the crucial Battle for Keren, flying standing patrols over our bombers. The Italian fighters seemed to be appearing in bigger and bigger numbers at more frequent intervals, and the bombers – Lysanders of 'A' Flight and 'C' Flight's Hardys – began suffering crippling losses. We joined the other flights in close support work, and ironically it was in this role that we got our first CR.42.'

The successful pilot was Flg Off Peter Simmonds, who's brother Rodney (himself a Spitfire pilot with Nos 238 and 94 Sqns, and credited with one Bf 109G destroyed over Italy – author) recalled to the author his brother's account of his combat of 16 March 1941, given during a home leave:

'I was stooging along with my flight commander Eric Smith when I heard a string of machine gun fire that perforated my mainplane. A little stunned, I could see nothing behind, so was wondering where the firing was coming from when a CR.42 climbed up in front of me and did a

77

perfect stall turn. I had little to do other than press the firing button, and down went the CR.42 in flames. Evidently the Italian pilots were "perfectionist" flyers who did all their manoeuvres according to the book!'

A month later Simmonds was escorting a Lysander to Debarech when he came across a lone S.79. The bomber pulled away, but not before he had opened fire and seen hits along the fuselage. At the end of the month he shared in the destruction of two Ca.133s, an S.79 and a CR.42 on the ground at Alomata and Cer-Cer. Peter Simmonds was No 237 Sqn's most successful Gladiator pilot. He was subsequently killed in Gladiator K7984 in Iraq on 14 April 1942 after the Rhodesians had converted to Hurricanes. Eric Smith, by then the CO, wrote:

'Peter was practically worshipped on the squadron – he always displayed dash with grim determined fighting spirit which always captured the imagination. To me personally the loss was a most grievous one.'

March 1941 saw 'K' Flight withdrawn to Palestine, whilst in Kenya, a shortage of Hurricanes meant that some Gladiators were issued to No 3 Sqn SAAF. Although there was still much hard fighting to be done in East Africa before the Italians finally surrendered in November, the old biplanes saw little further air combat.

Appropriately, however, the last Italian aircraft shot down in the campaign fell to a Gladiator. At 1735 hrs on 24 October, SottoTen Malavolti flew a recce in one of the two remaining CR.42s in-theatre. The SAAF at Dabat heard the Fiat overhead, and Lt L C H Hope took off in a Gladiator and spotted it about 1000 ft below him. The Italian took violent evasive action as Hope opened fire and closed to within 20 yards. There was

The RAF was not the only operator of the Gladiator during the Iraqi revolt of May 1941, for the Royal Iraqi Air Force operated nine Gloster fighters with No 4 Sqn. One shared in the destruction of an RAF Wellington, and another is believed to have been shot down by a Fighter Flight Gladiator near Baquba

In March 1941 No 94 Sqn again sent a detachment of Gladiators to Berbera to support the advance through British Somaliland. One of the aircraft despatched was N2287/GO-E, flown by Sgt L E Smith, seen here in sunglasses. His only success, albeit a notable one, was a Luftwaffe Bf 110 that he shot down over Iraq on 17 May (*Ian Simpson*)

a brief flicker of flame and the Fiat went in near Ambazzo – the last Italian aircraft shot down over East Africa. It was also the last claim by a Gladiator serving with a fighter unit.

THE IRAQ REBELLION

In April 1941, seizing the opportunity of Allied reverses in Greece and the desert, a pro-Axis coup led by Rashid Ali took place in Iraq. Invoking long-standing agreements, Imperial troops were landed at Basra at the head of the Red Sea. In reprisal on 29 April, a 9,000-strong Iraqi force invested the large RAF base at Habbaniya, to the west of Baghdad. Some reinforcement of the flying training school there had taken place, including the delivery of six Gladiators that joined three others in a Fighter Flight under the command of a Flt Lt May.

Amongst other preparations, No 94 Sqn in Egypt, which was converting to Hurricanes under the leadership of the now Wg Cdr Wightman, was ordered to collect five Gladiators from a maintenance unit and proceed to Habbaniya. Gladiators were also serving in the Royal Iraqi Air Force at the time as well, with nine being on strength with No 4 (Fighter) Sqn at Kirkuk.

Six of these aircraft attacked Habbaniya on 2 May, destroying three aircraft by strafing. In response, RAF aircraft attempting to defend the base ran the gauntlet of intense Iraqi ground fire. The Fighter Flight remained active, however, and several Iraqi attacks were disrupted. The following day saw further raids by Iraqi bombers, which were again opposed by RAF Gladiators. Flg Off Cleaver hit an S.79B, causing it to dive away pouring

Other than the CO, the only No 94 Sqn pilot to achieve more than one victory was Sgt Bill Dunwoodie. His second kill was a Bf 110 that he destroyed over Rashid on 17 May 1941. His victim exploded, so this photograph obviously shows Dunwoodie examining the wreckage of another ZG 26 aircraft after the ceasefire had come into effect (*author's collection*)

79

smoke – it crash-landed in the desert. Later that same day later Flt Lt May intercepted a formation of Northrop 8A-4s and damaged one, which also crash landed. Patrols continued over the base as RAF attacks on Iraqi airfields increased.

The 4th saw a Wellington shot down, shared by ground fire and a Gladiator of No 4 Sqn. However, the constant British attacks on the Iraqis took their toll, and a withdrawal commenced on the 6th from those areas still occupied within Habbaniya.

During a bomber escort to Baquba the following day, Plt Off Watson of the Fighter Flight had a unique combat when he was attacked by an Iraqi Gladiator. He fired at point blank range from astern and it is thought to have crashed not far from the target. That same day the detachment from No 94 Sqn prepared to move.

The Germans and Italians supported the Iraqis, and both sent small detachments, with Luftwaffe Bf 110s and He 111s flying in on 12 May. Four days later the He 111s of 4./KG 4 attacked Habbaniya for the first time. They were engaged by Flg Off Gerry Herrtage in L7616, who then became caught in crossfire. The incident was described in a letter from the flight commander to Herrtage's brother:

'We were doing a Standing Patrol over Habbaniya camp during the Iraqi rebellion when three Heinkels appeared, one of which Gerry engaged in a very spirited manner and shot it down. He broke away and attacked another one at close range and damaged it, but unfortunately one of their rear gunners put a bullet in his petrol tank which caused the Gladiator to blow up. Gerry bailed out, but unfortunately his parachute got tangled up somehow and did not open fully. He was killed instantly, and except for the few seconds falling, you need have no fear about his suffering.'

The day after this sad loss more of No 94 Sqn's aircraft arrived, and during a patrol over Rashid airfield Sgts Smith and Dunwoodie surprised two Bf 110s of 1./ZG 76 as they took off and both were shot down. Bill

On 6 June 1941 Gladiator I K6140 joined the little known unit 'X' Flight at Amman, which had been formed for the invasion of Syria. Its pilots tangled several times with Vichy Dewoitine D.520s, with the two claimed on 18 June being the last to fall to RAF Gladiators serving with a fighter unit (*M Hodgeson*)

Dunwoodie, who had one CR.42 to his name already, vividly described the action:

'At approximately 0755 hrs on 17 May 1941 we arrived over Rashid aerodrome, and after completing a half circuit of the airfield, I noticed two twin-engined machines in front of one of the hangars. One of these machines commenced to take off immediately, and both Sgt Smith and myself dived towards the aerodrome, only to see the second machine take off as well before we were in a position to attack. As soon as the aircraft left the ground, they did a steep climbing turn, and by then I observed Sgt Smith in engagement with one of them. I immediately engaged the second and a dogfight ensued. By this time I had identified the enemy as Me 110s.

'After a few minutes combat, in which I was able to get in a few short bursts with my guns, I observed one Me 110 flash past my port wing in a dive with masses of smoke pouring from both engines and Sgt Smith hot on its tail. A few seconds later I was able to get in an excellent astern attack on the other aircraft, putting a burst right up the fuselage. Almost immediately there was a terrific flash and the Me 110 became a mass of flame and disintegrated in the air. I then observed the one that Sgt Smith had shot down blazing furiously on the ground. The one that I had shot down was scattered over a wide area in pieces, all of which were ablaze. Both machines crashed within a half-mile of each other, approximately one mile south east of Rashid aerodrome.'

This must have been a shattering blow to German morale, although several days later Smith was lucky to escape with his life when he encountered the Bf 110s again. On 23 May 12 Italian CR.42s arrived in Iraq, and one of these was attacked by Wg Cdr Wightman six days later in what was to prove the final air-to-air engagement of the brief campaign. Freddie Wightman described his third confirmed kill thus:

'At 0930 hrs on 29 May 1941 I was escorting three Audax on a bombing raid on enemy positions at Khan Nuqta. Approaching the target, I saw an unidentified aircraft below me on my left. I found that it was a CR.42 with Iraqi markings when another one dived at me from above out of the sun with its guns firing. I turned quickly and evaded it by diving towards and under it, and it pulled up to a great height and repeated the manoeuvre. I repeated the evading action, and by turning quickly got in a burst whilst it was climbing up. It then went into a left-hand turn and there was no difficulty in turning inside it and keeping the sights on it, whilst the range was closing to 100 yards. After three bursts, black smoke poured from the engine and it went straight down. A second or two later the pilot escaped by parachute, and was captured by our troops. The aircraft was burnt out on crashing.'

The ceasefire of the following day just about brought an end to the Gladiator's fighter career in the RAF. A small unit, 'X' Flight, was formed on 6 June for service during the invasion of Syria, and it saw some action. On the 15th it became involved in a dogfight over Kissoue with Vichy D.520s, two of which were claimed for the loss of one Gladiator and another badly damaged. 'X' Flight bounced a formation of D.520s three days later, again over Kissoue, and this time claimed two for no loss. Although they served for a little while longer with the RAF in Iran, the days of the Gladiator as a frontline fighter in the air force had ended.

EPILOGUE

The fighting over Crete, Iraq and Syria in May-June 1941 effectively brought the Gladiator's career as a fighter to an end. A few were used in Egypt to perform tactical reconnaissance duties with No 6 Sqn, or relegated to second line tasks such at meteorological reconnaissance. The Finns also deployed the Gladiator in the tactical recce role during their 'Continuation War' against the Soviets. Used by LLv 16 in support of the Karelian Army initially during the advance around Lake Ladoga, to them went the distinction of the Gladiator's last kill.

Just after dark on 15 February 1943, 1Lt Hakan Stromberg (in GL-273) led GL-271 on a recce, checking on the stations, roads and airfields along the Murmansk railway between the White Sea and Lake Onega. His combat report relates the events:

'Karkijarvi 2005 hrs. Landing lights on in our style. One R-5 took off from the airfield. It was shot down in the forest next to the airfield with my second burst. Machine gun anti-aircraft fire from the airfield during my second dive.'

Thus in the remote Arctic fell the final victim of the Gloster Gladiator, a fighter which by rights really should not have seen much combat during World War 2. Nonetheless, it had been flown with great distinction and gallantry by many of the most able pilots of several nations, some of whom were amongst the leading aces of the conflict.

The last ever victory by a Gladiator was made by Finn 1Lt Hakan Stromberg (seen here sitting on the fighter's wing) of LLv 16 on 15 February 1943. He was flying this aircraft (GL-273), which appears to be wearing winter camouflage, at the time. Stromberg was subsequently killed on 7 April whilst flying this same machine when it crashed at Karkijarvella (*Kari Stenman*)

APPENDICES

APPENDIX 1

Commonwealth Gladiator Aces

Pilot	Service	Gladiator Score	Total Score	Gladiator Unit(s)
M T StJ Pattle	RAF	15.5/4/4	50+/8/6	80p/w
W Vale	RAF	10+2sh/-/1.5	30+3 sh/6/1	33p/w and 80
J F Fraser	RAF	9.5/-/2	9.5/-/2	112
D S Gregory	RAF	8/-/-	8/-/-	33p and 80
C E Casbolt	RAF	7.5/1/1.5	13.5/1/4	80
H P Cochrane	RAF	7/2/1	7/2/1	112
Alan H Boyd	RAAF	6/2/1	6.5/2/3	3 RAAF
G M Donaldson	RAF	6/2/-	6/2/-	112
R N Cullen	RAF	6/1/1	15/2/1	80
L G Schwab	RAF	6/1/-	6/1/-	80p and 112
V C Woodward	RAF	4+2sh/-/-	18+4sh/3/4	33
A T Williams	RAF	1+5sh/-/- (+1.5 unconfirmed destroyed)	1+5sh/-/- (+1.5 unconfirmed destroyed)	263
V A J Stuckey	RAF	5.5/1/-	5.5/1/-	80
E G Jones	RAF	5/-/-	5/-/-	80
H H Kitchener	RAF	5sh/-/1	5sh/-/2	263
J L Groves	RAF	4.5/2/2	6.5/2/3	112
C B Hull	RAF	4.5/-/2 (+1.5 unconfirmed destroyed)	4+4sh/2.5/2 (+1.5 unconfirmed destroyed)	263
R A Acworth	RAF	4.5/1/1	7.5/1/2	112

Notes (also applicable to following appendices):

– Scores split as follows – confirmed destroyed/probably destroyed/damaged

– P after unit indicates pre-war service

– W after unit indicates wartime service

APPENDIX 2

Commonwealth Aces with Gladiator Claims

Pilot	Service	Gladiator Score	Total Score	Gladiator Unit(s)
W S Arthur	RAAF	2/-/1	8/2/6	3 RAAF
N Bowker	RAF	1/3/1	10/4/2	112
B J L Boyle	SAAF	3/-/-	5.5/-/-	1 SAAF
G Burges	RAF	3/-/2	7/2/6	Hal Far Ftr Flt and 261
L Cottingham	RAF	4/-/-	11.5/1/2	80p and 33
E H Dean	RAF	2/-/-	5/-/2	80p and 33
A Duncan	SAAF	2 (+4 on gnd)/-/-	5.5/1/10	1 SAAF
P H Dunn	RAF	3/-/-	6+3 sh/2/1.5	80
A D Forster	RAuxF	-/-/3	6/-/4.5	607
C H Fry	RAAF	4/2/1	5/2/1	112
E W F Hewett	RAF	3/-/-	16/2/-	80
J L Hewitson	SAAF	1/-/-	5/-/1	1 SAAF
C L Keighly-Peach	RN	3.5/1/-	3.5/1/-	813 Ftr Flt/HMS *Eagle*
G V W Kettlewell	RAF	3/1/-	5/1/-	80
G J Le Mesurier	SAAF	1/-/1	3/1/1	1 SAAF
S Linnard	RAF	2/2/1	6.5/3/5	80
R Pare	SAAF	1.5/-/-	6/1/3	1 SAAF
D G Parnall	RAF	1/-/-	2+4 sh/2/1	263
J R Perrin	RAAF	-/1/-	6/1/-	3 RAAF
A C Rawlinson	RAAF	-/1/3	8/2/8	3 RAAF
W Riley	RAF	1.5/-/-	9+3 sh/2/1	263
J G Sanders	RAuxAF	-/-/1	16/1/6	615
J E Scoular	RAF	1/-/-	14+3 sh/1/3	73p and 'K' Flt
A J Sewell	RN	1.5/-/-	6+7 sh/1/3	806
G H Steege	RAAF	3/2/1	8/2/5	3 RAAF
P StG B Turnbull	RAAF	-/1/1	12/1/2	3 RAAF
J L Waters	RAF	2/-/-	4 (poss 6)/-/1	Hal Far Ftr Flt
D F Westenra	RAF	2/-/2	8+3 sh/2/4	112
B E P Whall	RAF	1/-/-	7+2 sh/2/-	263
P R W Wickham	RAF	4/-/-	10/7/15	3p 33p/w and 112
T S Wildblood	RAF	.5/-/-	3+2 sh/-/-	152
W J Woods	RAF	2.5/1/1	6.5/2/1	Hal Far Ftr Flt, 261 and 80
P G Wykeham-Barnes	RAF	3.5/-/-	14+3 sh/1/2	80p/w

APPENDIX 3

Aces Who Flew Gladiators but made no Claims

Pilot	Service	Total Score	Gladiator Unit(s)
G Allard	RAF	19+5 sh/2/-	87p
D H Allen	RAF	3+3 sh/-/-	85p
J L Allen	RAF	7.5/-/-	54p
A B Angus	RAF	5/-/-	85p
H W Ayre	RAF	5/2/-	769p and 804w
A W A Bayne	RAF	7+4 sh/2+4sh/2	54p
G T Baynham	RAF	5+2 sh/-/-	80p/w
J M Bazin	RAuxAF	4 (poss 10)/1/1	607p/w
The Hon W Beaumont	RAF	6+2 sh/-/2	152w
W F Blackadder	RAuxAF	2+5 sh/-/3	607p/w
K H Blair	RAF	5+2 sh/5.5/3	85p
J C Boulter	RAF	4 or 5/3.5//1	72p and 603w
Adrian H Boyd	RAF	15+3 sh/2/4	65p
J M Bruen	RN	4+4 sh/-/2+2sh	801p and 769p
P A Burnell-Phillips	RAF	5/.5/-	54p, 65p and 607w
C R Bush	RAuxAF	3.5/2/3	615w
E J Cain	RAF	16/-/1	73p
B J G Carbury	RAF	15+2 sh/2/5	603w
J M V Carpenter	RAF	8/1/3	263w
J H Coghlan	RAF	3.5/-/6	72p
P Collard	RAuxAF	1.5 (poss 6)/1/2	615p/w
R J Cork	RN	9+2 sh/1/4	759w
D Crowley-Milling	RAF	4.5/2/1.5	615w
R Dahl	RAF	5/-/-	80w
E C Deanesly	RAF	4+2 sh/-/-	605p and 152w
A C Deere	RAF	17.5/4/7.5	54p
G L Denholm	RAuxAF	3+3 sh/3.5/6	603p/w
H P Dixon	RAuxAF	3+2 sh/-/2	607p/w
E M Donaldson	RAF	5.5 (poss 8.5)/-/1	72p
W A Douglas	RAuxAF	6/2.5/7	603p/w
J J Doyle	RCAF	5/1/4	Comms Unit Western Desert
C H Dyson	RAF	9/-/-	33p/w
G R Edge	RAuxAF	20/3/7	605p
T A F Elsdon	RAF	7/-/2	72p
A Eyre	RAuxAF	8+2 sh/2/6	615p/w
L M Gaunce	RAF	5.5/2.5/6	3p
G K Gilroy	RAuxAF	14+10 sh/2sh/5+4sh	603p/w
J B Hobbs	RAF	4+3 sh/-/-	3p
F J Howell	RAF	7+3 sh/2/2.5	80p
P H Hugo	RAF	17+3 sh/2/2.5	615w
J B W Humpherson	RAF	5/2/3	72p/607w
R J Hyde	RAF	5/1/1	769p
J F Jackson	RAAF	7/1/-	3 RAAF
C G StD Jeffries	RAF	4+2 sh/3/2	261w
P Jeffery	RAAF	5.5/-/1	3 RAAF
J R Kayll	RAuxAF	7.5 (poss 12.5)/2/6	607p/w and 615w
C B F Kingcome	RAF	8+3 sh/5/13	65p
J H Lapsley	RAF	11/-/-	80p/w
J A Leathart	RAF	7.5/2/3	54p
R H A Lee	RAF	9/-/- approx	85p

K T Lofts	RAuxAF	4+3 sh (poss 7+3 sh)/1/5.5	615p/w
J A F Maclachlan	RAF	16.5/1/3	261w
E M Mason	RAF	15+2 sh/-/3+3 sh	80p/w, 261w and Iraq
H D McGregor	RAF	6/-/- or 2/-/2?	33p/w
P F Morfill	RAF	6.5/-/4	65p
T C Morris	RAF	3+2 sh/-/3 sh	80p/w
J S Morton	RAuxAF	6+4 sh/5/6	603p/w
N Orton	RAF	17/8/3.5	73p
P L Parrott	RAF	5+4 sh/1/5+2 sh	607w
G F Powell-Sheddon	RAF	4+2 sh/2 sh/-	33w
F N Robertson	RAF	11.5/3/7	261W
J H W Saunders	RAAF	6/-/2	3 RAAF
D F B Sheen	RAF	4.5/2/2	72p
F M Smith	RAF	2.5/1/1	72p
J D Smith	RAF	7.5/1/2	87p
H J Starrett	RAF	3+3 sh/2/-	33w
C A C Stone	RAF	5+2 sh/-/2	3p
K N V Townsend	RAuxAF	3+2 sh/-/1	607p/w
R R S Tuck	RAF	27+2 sh/6/6.5	65p
J W Villa	RAF	13+4 sh/4/4	72p
R Voase-Jeff	RAF	4 (+1 unconfirmed)/-/-	87p
R C Wilkinson	RAF	7+2 sh/-/1	3p

APPENDIX 4

Finnish Gladiator Aces

Name/Rank	Gladiator Score	Total Score	Gladiator Unit
O E K Tuominen/SSgt	6.5/-/1	44/-/1	LLv 26
P D Berg/Lt	5/-/1	9.5/-/1	LLv 26
A I Joensuu/Cpl	4	5	LLv 26
L J Lautamaki/WO	2.5	5.5	LLv 26
V V Porvari/SSgt	2	7.5	LLv 26
S Suikanen/Sgt	1	4.5	LLv 26

APPENDIX 5

Chinese Gladiator Aces

Name/Rank	Gladiator Claims	Total Score	Gladiator Unit
Shi-Tin Chin/Capt	6.5/-/2.5	8.5/-/2.5	28 FS
Wong Sun-Shui/Maj	5/-/1.5	7/-/2.5	29 FS
Louie Yim-Qun/Maj	2+2 sh/-/1	2+2 sh/-/1	28FS
Wong Pan-Yang/Lt Col	1+3 sh/-/-	4+5 sh/-/1	5th Air Group
Zhu Jia-Xun/Capt	2/-/1	5/-/1	32 FS
Teng Chung-kai	2/-/.5	2+2 sh/-/.5	29 FS

APPENDIX 6

Leading Gladiator Pilots of Minor Users

Belgian Army Air Service

Name/Rank	Gladiator Claims	Gladiator Unit
Henri Winand/1Sgt	-/-/1	*1éme Esc de Chasse* 'la Comete'
Denys Rolin/1Sgt	-/-/1	*1éme Esc de Chasse* 'la Comete'

Royal Hellenic Air Force

Name/Rank	Gladiator Claims	Total Score	Gladiator Unit
Ionnis Kellas/Capt	2/-/-	3/-/-	21 *Mira*
Anastassios Bardivilias/2Lt	2/-/-	2/-/-	21 *Mira*

Norwegian Air Service Fighter Wing

Name/Rank	Gladiator Claims	Gladiator Unit
Dag Krohn/Lt	2/-/1	*Jagevingen*
Kristian Fredrik Schye/Sgt	1/-/-	*Jagevingen*
Finn Thorsager/2Lt	1/-/-	*Jagevingen*
Rolf Thorjorn Tradin/Lt	1/-/-	*Jagevingen*
Per Waaler/Sgt	1/-/-	*Jagevingen*

Royal Swedish Air Force (*Flygvapnet*)

Name/Rank	Gladiator Claims	Total Score	Gladiator Unit
Per-Johan Salwen/2Lt	3/-/1 (+1.5 unconfirmed destroyed)	3/-/1 (+1.5 unconfirmed destroyed)	*Flygflottilj* F 19
Einar Tehler/2Lt	2/-/-	2/-/-	*Flygflottilj* F 19
Gidden Karlsson/2Lt	1/-/1	1/-/1	*Flygflottilj* F 19
Arne Frykholm/2Lt	2 sh/-/-	2 sh/-/-	*Flygflottilj* F 19
Carl-Olaf Steninger/2Lt	2 sh/-/-	2 sh/-/-	*Flygflottilj* F 19
Ian Iacobi/2Lt	1/-/-	1/-/-	*Flygflottilj* F 19
Roland Martin/2Lt	1/-/-	1/-/-	*Flygflottilj* F 19

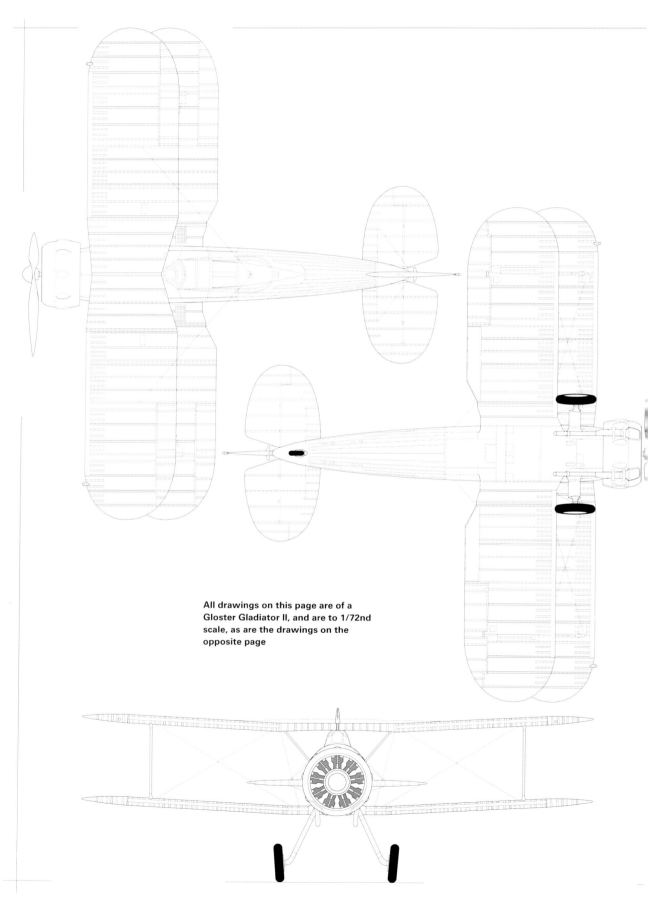

All drawings on this page are of a
Gloster Gladiator II, and are to 1/72nd
scale, as are the drawings on the
opposite page

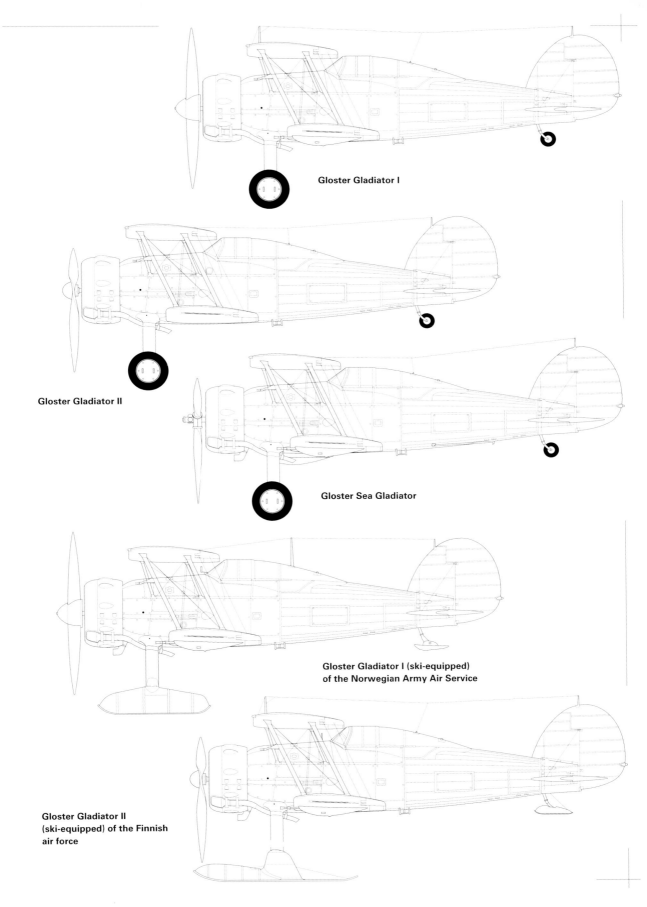

Gloster Gladiator I

Gloster Gladiator II

Gloster Sea Gladiator

Gloster Gladiator I (ski-equipped)
of the Norwegian Army Air Service

Gloster Gladiator II
(ski-equipped) of the Finnish
air force

1

Gladiator II N5851 of No 6 Sqn, flown by Sgt Ron Walter, Kufra Oasis, Egypt, 21 September 1941

The distinction of claiming the RAF's final Gladiator kill went to Sgt Ron Walter who, flying N5851, shot down an Italian S.81 near Kufra Oasis on 26 September 1941. 'C' Flight had been detached there from the unit's base at Wadi Halfa for almost a month, and Kufra had received several 'visits' from both the Luftwaffe and the *Regia Aeronautica* during this time. This was Walter's only air combat claim, and a rare kill for No 6 Sqn, which later specialised in 'tank busting'.

2

Gladiator I K8013 of No 33 Sqn, flown by Sqn Ldr Hector McGregor, Ramleh, Palestine, late 1938

The Gladiator first saw active service with the RAF in Palestine in 1938, when elements of No 33 Sqn supported Army policing operations during fighting between Arabs and Jews. The unit's aircraft were often employed on air cordon operations around villages, and were occasionally hit or even brought down by groundfire. McGregor was awarded a DSO for his leadership during this period, his aircraft (K8013), although not yet wearing unit code letters, is carrying his squadron leader's rank pennant under the cockpit. This machine later served with No 80 Sqn, and was eventually transferred to the Greeks in 1941. In early 1940, McGregor returned to the UK, where he led No 213 Sqn during the Battle of Britain, and was reportedly credited with six destroyed.

3

Gladiator I K8036 of No 33 Sqn, flown by Sgt Bill Vale, Ramleh, Palestine, early 1939

An NCO pilot during the fighting in Palestine, Bill 'Cherry' Vale of No 33 Sqn flew this aircraft whilst participating in the policing action. Although it wears the squadron's code letters, the Gladiator does not yet have an individual aircraft letter or camouflage. It later served with No 80 and 267 Sqns. Vale, with 30 and 3 shared destroyed in total, was one of the RAF's leading (but least known) aces. He made his first claim, a CR.32, over Fort Capuzzo whilst flying N5769 on 1 July 1940. Soon afterwards he transferred to No 80 Sqn, with whom he made the rest of his kills – these included 10 and 2 shared on Gladiators, making him second only to Pattle on the type.

4

Gladiator I L7619 of No 33 Sqn, flown by Plt Off Vernon Woodward, Ismailia, Egypt, circa June 1939

In the spring of 1939 changes were made to unit code letters within the RAF, No 33 Sqn's becoming TN, as displayed on L7619, which also wears a temporary 'desert' camouflage scheme. It was flown on occasion from Ismailia by 23-year-old Canadian Plt Off Vernon Woodward, who, on 14 June 1940, participated in No 33 Sqn's first decisive combat against the Italians – he shared in the destruction of a Caproni Ca.310. Woodward shot down another five aircraft (one shared) over the next five weeks flying Gladiators. L7619 later served in the Sudan with 'K' Flight.

5

Gladiator II N5782 of No 33 Sqn, flown by Flg Off E H Dean, Mersa Matruh, Egypt, 14 June 1940

Although some sources record his aircraft as L9046, it is believed that on the morning of 14 June 1940, Flg Off Ernest Dean was flying this Gladiator over Fort Capuzzo when he shot down the CR.32 flown by Sgt Azzaroni of 8° *Gruppo*, thus claiming No 33 Sqn's first victory. Although having served with the squadron since new, the fighter does not wear any unit codes (possibly following repainting), and it is understood not to have done so in this historic combat. N5782 was later coded NW-G, and eventually transferred to No 3 Sqn RAAF, where it was used by aces Alan Boyd to destroy two CR.42s on 13 December and Alan Rawlinson to claim a probable on Boxing Day 1940.

6

Gladiator II N5784 of No 33 Sqn, flown by Flg Off Vernon Woodward, Helwan, Egypt, August 1940

One of the RAF's leading aces of World War 2, 'Woody' Woodward made all his 18 destroyed and 4 shared claims whilst serving with No 33 Sqn in 1940-41. Four of his victories and two shares came whilst flying Gladiators – he shared a Ca.310 and may have downed a CR.32 on 14 June whilst flying N5783, and brought down two CR.32s on the 29th. His final Gladiator claims were made on 25 July, when he shot down a CR.42 and shared in the destruction of another. Woodward was then pulled back to Helwan with the rest of his unit, where, amongst others, he flew this aircraft. This may have been the Gladiator he took back to Gerawla on 16 August to cover the return of a Royal Navy force that had just shelled Bardia. Although other units found action on this date, No 33 Sqn was not engaged, and soon re-equipped with Hurricanes. N5784 appears to have worn the four-colour shadow-compensating scheme, but otherwise had standard markings.

7

Gladiator I K8015 of 'B' Flight No 65 Sqn, flown by Plt Off Robert Stanford Tuck, Hornchurch, early 1938

Amongst the many pilots who flew Gladiators before World War 2 and later became aces, perhaps Bob Tuck was the most prominent. After flying training, he joined No 65 Sqn at Hornchurch in May 1936, initially flying Gauntlets, and, from June 1937, the Gladiator. With Flt Lt Bicknall (as leader) and Sgt Percy Morfill (flying K8013) as number three, he flew formation aerobatics in this aircraft at several air shows in 1938. Tuck was shot down by flak over France in January 1942 and he spent the rest of the war as a PoW.

8

Gladiator I K6142 of 'B' Flight No 72 Sqn, flown by Plt Off J B Humpherson, Church Fenton, mid-1937

The first RAF Gladiator squadron was No 72, which re-formed with the Gloster fighters in February 1937. It soon numbered amongst its pilots men who would attain distinction during the coming war. One such individual was John Humpherson, who flew with No 72 Sqn until August 1939, when he was transferred to No 607 Sqn. He duly flew Gladiators with the auxiliary unit in France. During the course of 1940 Humpherson destroyed five aircraft whilst flying Hurricanes with Nos 607 and 32 Sqns, and was awarded a DFC at the end of August. Transferred to No 90 Sqn in May 1941, he was killed the following month when his Fortress I bomber broke up in mid-air and crashed.

9
Gladiator I K7985 of No 73 Sqn, flown by Plt Off E G Kain, Digby, 1937
Famous as the RAF's first ace of World War 2, New Zealander 'Cobber' Kain joined Gladiator-equipped No 73 Sqn after completing his flying training and flew formation aerobatics at the 1938 Empire Air Day. For a time his aircraft was K7985, which wore No 73's distinctive markings prior to it being transferred to No 3 Sqn on 30 March 1938. Kain remained with No 73 Sqn after its re-equipment with Hurricanes, and had already shot down five German aircraft by the time the Battle of France began on 10 May 1940. By the time of his death (in a flying accident) on 6 June, his score had risen to 16 destroyed and one damaged.

10
Gladiator I K7903 of No 80 Sqn, flown by Flt Lt E G Jones, Ismailia, Egypt, circa June 1939
K7903 was delivered to No 80 Sqn on 9 April 1937, and served with the squadron until being shot down by CR.42s on 8 August 1940. For a long time it was the aircraft of 'Tap' Jones, 'A' Flight commander, who initially had it decorated with a red fin and unit badge. K7903 later received the unit codes OD, becoming aircraft B, and then GK-B when the codes were changed in April 1939. Following the outbreak of war it became YK-B. Its pilot, who later became Air Marshal Sir Edward Jones, shot down all five of his victories with the Gladiator, the first falling on 27 November 1940. All of his successes were against CR.42s.

11
Gladiator I K8011 of No 80 Sqn, flown by Flg Off John Lapsley, Amriya, Egypt, late 1939
Another of No 80 Sqn's pilots to rise to air marshal was John Lapsley, who flew Gladiators with the squadron from 1938, until joining the squadron's Hurricane Flight, which quickly became No 274 Sqn. All of his 11 kills were claimed flying Hurricanes. By late 1939 No 80 Sqn was again experimenting with desert camouflage schemes, as is evident with Lapsley's aircraft, which wears No 80 Sqn's wartime code letters YK. Delivered to the squadron on 18 August 1937, K8011 remained with the unit for over three years, and was eventually stuck off charge in June 1941.

12
Gladiator I L8011 of No 80 Sqn, flown by Flt Lt M T StJ Pattle, Amriya, Egypt, early 1940
Part of a batch of 28, L8011 served with No 80 Sqn until it was eventually transferred to the Greeks. It was flown regularly by 'Pat' Pattle in the spring of 1940, retaining its green and brown camouflage and black/white undersides. Pattle's first combat with the Italians took place near El Adem on 4 August 1940, during which he was forced to bail out of

K7910 after making his first claims – a Ba.65 and a CR.32. He went on to become the RAF's leading scorer, with a total of around 50 victories – 15.5 of these were claimed with the Gladiators. Pattle was the greatest exponent of the vintage biplane, the bulk of his claims being made over Greece; his final Gladiator kill being a CR.42 over Tepelene on 9 February 1941.

13
Gladiator I K7973 of No 80 Sqn, flown by Plt Off G K Baynham, Amriya, Egypt, 26 March 1940
Plt Off Geoffrey Baynham was flying K7973 on the night of 26 March 1940 when, during an attempted overshoot at No 80 Sqn's base at Amriya, he suffered a loss of power and hit the ground. The aircraft, which had originally served with No 73 Sqn, before joining No 80 in 1938, was badly damaged, but after repair it was transferred to the Royal Hellenic Air Force in December 1940. Baynham returned to the UK and later flew Spitfires, initially with No 234 Sqn and later with No 152. Between 1941 and 1943 he shot down seven German aircraft (two shared), and in one combat, on 17 July 1941, destroyed three Bf 109s over the Channel.

14
Gladiator I L8009 of No 80 Sqn, flown by Flg Off Peter Wykeham-Barnes, Sidi Barrani, Egypt, 4 August 1940
Flying this aircraft late in the afternoon of 4 August 1940 whilst leading a four-aircraft formation, Peter Wykeham-Barnes attacked and shot down a Breda Ba.65 of Italian 159° *Squadriglia* to claim No 80 Sqn's first Gladiator kill. In the ensuing combat, he was hit by fire from a CR.32 and forced to bail out. Wykeham-Barnes was picked up by British troops the following day. He went on to attain ace status with a final score of 14 and 3 shared destroyed, of which 3.5 were claimed whilst flying Gladiators. His aircraft in this combat retained black and white undersides, which was a recognition feature.

15
Gladiator II N2287 of No 94 Sqn, flown by Sgt L E Smith, Berbera, British Somaliland, March 1941
The main fighter defence for Aden was provided by Gladiators of No 94 Sqn, the unit also protecting the port of Berbera, in British Somaliland. After the allied re-occupation of the latter territory in 1941, desert-camouflaged Gladiators of No 94 Sqn were again based in the colony, including this aircraft of Sgt L E Smith. Its pilot made no claims during the East African campaign, but secured a notable scalp over Iraq when he shot down a Bf 110 of 1./ZG 76 over Rashid for his only kill.

16
Gladiator I K7974 of 'B' Flight No 112 Sqn, flown by Plt Off P O V Green, Gedaref, Sudan, 1 August 1940
Camouflaged in 'European' colours, with black and white undersides, this aircraft was used by Plt Off Green to claim the squadron's second kill over the Sudan when he brought down a Caproni Ca.133. The detachment of No 112 Sqn was re-titled 'K' Flight shortly afterwards. K7974 originally served in England with Nos 87 and 72 Sqns but was written off with 'K' Flight when it swung on take-off at Port Sudan on 22 December 1940.

17

Gladiator II (serial unknown) of No 112 Sqn, flown by Sqn Ldr L G Schwab, Paramythia, Greece, April 1941

No 112 Sqn's Gladiators had many successes against the Italians over Greece during the late winter and spring of 1941. One of the leading exponents was 'Algy' Schwab, who made all his claims flying Gladiators with No 112 Sqn, the first being an S.79 on 17 August 1940. On 4 April 1941, he became squadron CO, making his final claim (probably destroying a G.50) on the 13th, when he is believed to have been flying this aircraft.

18

Gladiator II N5815 of No 237 'Rhodesia' Sqn, flown by Flg Off Peter Simmonds, Asmara, Eritrea, 29 April 1941

In late February 1941 'B' Flight of the Rhodesian-manned No 237 Sqn received ex-SAAF Gladiators, including this one, which were used mainly for ground attack work. However, one CR.42 was destroyed and an S.79 damaged, both by Flg Off Simmonds, for his only air combat claims. Flying this aircraft on 29 and 30 April during ground strafing attacks on Alamata, he shared in the damage or destruction of a number of Italian aircraft. N5815 did not survive long, however, being wrecked in a crash at Asmara on 25 May 1941.

19

Gladiator II N5682 of No 247 Sqn, flown by Sqn Ldr P G O'Brien, Roborough, December 1940

The only Gladiator squadron to serve during the Battle of Britain was No 247, which had been created out of the Shetland Fighter Flight. Whilst flying Gladiators, No 247 Sqn fortunately experienced only one fleeting encounter with the Luftwaffe. Its CO was Canadian Sqn Ldr P G O'Brien, who flew 'K', for this was the aircraft letter of his godfather's Camel during World War 1. O'Brien later distinguished himself as the leader of the Spitfire-equipped Portreath Wing in 1943.

20

Sea Gladiator N5520 of No 261 Sqn, flown by Flt Lt C G StJ Jeffries, Takali, Malta, September 1941

After replacement in the fighter role, Gladiator N5520 (a veteran of the 1940 fighting) was used for meteorological reconnaissance duties on Malta. During this period it was flown by pilots of the various squadrons on the embattled island, including ace Flt Lt 'Porky' Jeffries of No 185 Sqn. He made his first trip in it on 1 September 1941, and logged at least another five sorties over the next month, all in this aircraft. N5520 now resides in the Malta National War Museum, having been used by Flg Off John Waters in the initial contact with the Italians on 11 June 1940.

21

Gladiator II N5905 of No 263 Sqn, flown by Sgt H H Kitchener, Bardufoss, Norway, 2 June 1940

Sadly, details of the aircraft flown by the gallant pilots of No 263 Sqn in Norway in the spring of 1940 are very scarce. However, it is known that N5905 was flown by surviving ace Herbert Kitchener, who shared the destruction of a Ju 90 in May. On 2 June he 'made ace' in company with Flt Lt Alvin Williams when, during several combats, the pair were credited with three He 111s and a Ju 87 destroyed, Kitchener also claiming a Ju 87 damaged. He later flew Whirlwinds with No 263 Sqn, claiming a Ju 88 damaged, before being severely injured in a crash following combat.

22

Gladiator I K7995 of No 607 'County of Durham' Sqn, flown by Flt Lt John Sample, Acklington, 17 October 1939

The first confirmed victory for a British-based Gladiator went to the auxiliaries of the 'County of Durham' squadron when three aircraft, led by former estate agent John Sample, brought down a Do 18 flying boat off the Northumberland coast. The German pilot had been told that his 'opposition' would comprise 'biplanes flown by barristers' – on being picked up he was mortified! Sample served with No 607 Sqn in France, and then became OC No 504 Sqn upon his return to England. He subsequently led the 'County of Nottingham' squadron during the Battle of Britain, ending the campaign with 1 and 2 shared destroyed. Posted away from the unit in March of the following year, Sample was killed in a mid-air collision near Bath while flying a Whirlwind as OC No 137 Sqn in October 1941. Gladiator K7995 later flew in the communications role in Egypt.

23

Gladiator I K7949 of No 615 'County of Surrey' Sqn, flown by Plt Off Tony Eyre, Ford, August 1939

The auxiliary Gladiator squadrons contained many future aces in their ranks including Plt Off Eyre, who claimed 8 and 2 shared destroyed flying Hurricanes with No 615 Sqn in the summer of 1940. During the summer of 1939 he flew this aircraft on several occasions, including on 26 June and 1-2 July. It wears the toned-down markings introduced at the time of the Munich Crisis, as well as No 615 Sqn's pre-war unit code letters RR. K7949 later served in Palestine on 'Met Recce' duties, before catching fire and being abandoned on 27 March 1942.

24

Gladiator II N2308 of No 615 'County of Surrey' Sqn, flown by Flt Lt James Sanders, Merville, France, 29 December 1939

The only validated claim by a RAF Gladiator over France was made by No 615 Sqn's flight commander, 'Sandy' Sanders, who damaged a He 111 on 29 December 1939 for his first claim. During the summer of 1940 he would be credited with at least 16 aircraft destroyed whilst flying Hurricanes with the 'County of Surrey' squadron – he also claimed a He 111 probably destroyed and a Ju 88 damaged flying Defiant nightfighters with No 253 Sqn in March and April 1941. This particular aircraft was evacuated from France to Kenley by another future ace, Flg Off Tony Eyre, on 22 May 1940. It later served with No 247 Sqn during the Battle of Britain.

25

Gladiator II N2312 of No 615 ('County of Surrey') Sqn, flown by Flg Off P H Hugo, St Inglevert, France, March 1940

One of many South Africans to join the RAF before World War 2, 'Dutch' Hugo arrived at No 615 Sqn straight from training in December 1939. He was to become a successful fighter pilot, claiming 17 and 3 shared victories. Hugo made no claims with the Gladiator, having converted to Hurricanes before the German *blitzkrieg*. He flew this aircraft, which later served on anti-aircraft co-operation duties, on a number of occasions, the first being a patrol on 10 March 1940.

26
Gladiator I K6134 of 'K' Flight, flown by Flt Lt J E Scoular, Port Sudan, Sudan, circa late 1940
A pre-war Gladiator pilot with No 73 Sqn, John Scoular achieved at least 12.5 kills with the unit flying Hurricanes during the Battle of France. He later assumed command of 'K' Flight, and made his only Gladiator kill on 22 February 1941 when he bounced an S.79 near Massawa. This also proved to be the last air combat claim for this small unit, for soon afterwards it moved to Palestine and formed the nucleus of No 250 Sqn, with Scoular as CO.

27
Sea Gladiator N5519 of the Hal Far Fighter Flight, flown by Flt Lt George Burges, Hal Far, Malta, June 1940
The most famous exploits of the RAF's Gladiators were undoubtedly those of the fabled defenders of Malta. One of the Sea Gladiators transferred from Navy charge was N5519, which like the others wears naval camouflage. Flying this aircraft on 22 June 1940, Flt Lt George Burges, who was originally a flying boat pilot, shot down S.79 MM22068 of 34° *Stormo* to claim the first confirmed victory by the Flight. He then brought down a C.200 the very next day, also in this aircraft. Burges went on to claim seven kills, of which three came flying Gladiators. N5519 did not survive long, however, being shot down by a CR.42 on 31 July.

28
Gladiator II N5752 of No 3 Sqn RAAF, flown by Flg Off A H Boyd, Gerawala, Egypt, 19 November 1940
This RAAF squadron partially re-equipped with ex-No 33 Sqn Gladiators in October 1940, and it took them into combat for the first time on 19 November 1940 in an epic action in which Alan Boyd claimed three CR.42s destroyed and a fourth as a probable. Eventually downing six CR.42s, he became the only RAAF Gladiator ace. Boyd later flew Kittyhawks over New Guinea, where he added a shared Zero to his score. This Gladiator retains No 33 Sqn's NW code letters, and wears a 'winged crown' badge forward of the cockpit. Flg Off 'Woof' Arthur also used N5752 to destroy a Fiat on 12 December.

29
Gladiator II L9044 of No 3 Sqn RAAF, flown by Flg Off Peter Turnbull, Martuba, Libya, 25 January 1941
This Gladiator II was originally N5889 prior to it being transferred to the Royal Egyptian Air Force as L9044. It retained this serial following its repossession by the RAF in the autumn of 1940. Note that the roundels and code letters added following its return were smaller than usual. In RAAF service, L9044 was used on 19 November by Flg Off Alan Rawlinson to claim a probable CR.42. The fighter also participated in No 3 Sqn's final combat with the Gladiator on 25 January 1941, future 12-victory ace Flg Off Peter Turnbull damaging a G.50 with it. By this time it bore the sobriquet *SWEET SUE*, surrounded by musical notes.

30
Gladiator II N5852 of No 1 Sqn SAAF, flown by Capt B J L Boyle, Azzoza, Eritrea, October 1940
'Piggy' Boyle was a flight commander with No 1 Sqn SAAF, and he was also one of the first South Africans to fly the Gladiator. Whilst at the controls of this aircraft over Eritrea on 4 October 1940, he was wounded in an attack by a CR.42, but he nevertheless succeeded in damaging a second Fiat fighter, which was later confirmed as having crashed. Boyle had scored his first victory. A month later, on 4 November, he was again flying N5852 in support of the attack on Fort Gallabat when he claimed his second kill by shooting down another CR.42. Two days later, Boyle hastily scrambled in this aircraft in a brave attempt to save his CO, who had been set upon by a formation of CR.42s. He arrived too late, however, and was wounded once again in the ensuing dogfight which only ended when he crash-landed N5852 – the fighter was destroyed. Boyle's three kills made him the leading SAAF Gladiator pilot.

31
Sea Gladiator N2272 of 804 NAS, flown by Sub Lt J W Sleigh, Hatston, Orkney, July 1940
A South African serving in the Royal Navy, 'Jimmy' Sleigh joined Sea Gladiator-equipped 804 NAS straight from training in June 1940, and served with the unit until November. 'His' aircraft, seen here, was unusual in that it wore a personal marking beneath the cockpit. Although he did not become an ace, Sleigh had several notable successes in 1941 flying Martlets with 802 NAS. Whilst detached in HMS *Victorious* in October he shared in the destruction of a He 111 and damaged another, and on 19 December, flying from the first escort carrier, HMS *Audacity*, he brought down an Fw 200 Condor. He later led a Naval Fighter Wing and served in Korea. Sleigh's awards included the DSO, OBE and DSC.

32
Sea Gladiator N5513 of 806 NAS, flown by Sub Lt A J Sewell, HMS *Illustrious*, 8 November 1940
This aircraft was one of two Sea Gladiators transferred from HMS *Eagle* to Fulmar-equipped 806 NAS to supplement the fighter defences of the recently arrived carrier HMS *Illustrious*. On 8 November N5513, flown by rising star 'Jackie' Sewell, was joined by Sub Lt Roger Nichols in N5549 to destroy a reconnaissance Cant Z.501 flying boat of 186° *Squadriglia*. This share was Sewell's first claim with the biplane, although he had already scored 3 and 2 shared victories whilst flying Fulmars during the preceding two months. On 24 January 1941, Sewell shot down a Ju 88 over Malta whilst flying a Sea Gladiator – the type's final claim over the battered island.

33
Sea Gladiator N5517 of 813 NAS Fighter Flight, flown by Cdr C L Keighly-Peach, HMS *Eagle*, July 1940
HMS *Eagle*'s fighter flight, which formed in June 1940 with four Sea Gladiators, was led by the ship's Commander (Flying), Cdr Charles Keighly-Peach. Under him the Flight prospered over the succeeding weeks, destroying possibly as many as seven Italian bombers – 'K-P' got most of them, for which he received a DSO. All of his five claims were made

flying this aircraft, which the following year served in Crete with 805 NAS, but was lost with its pilot when it force-landed in the sea south of the island on 15 May.

34

Gladiator I 2909 of the 29th FS/5th FLG (Chinese Air Force), flown by Maj 'John' Wong Pan-Yang, Xiaoquan, China, 16 June 1938

The Gladiator's combat debut came during the Sino-Japanese war on 24 February 1938 in an action against Japanese seaplanes at Nan-hsung, although due to a fuel leak 2909 did not actually get airborne. Possibly used in action on 13 April, 2909 definitely engaged the enemy on 16 June, when Maj 'John' Wong intercepted six G3M 'Nell' bombers. Wong, who already had 3 and 2 shared destroyed claims to his credit with the Boeing 281 'Peashooter', shot down one by diving and firing as he pulled up – the 'Nell's bomb load exploded, destroying the aircraft, but also damaging Wong's aircraft. Nonetheless, he was duly credited with sharing in the destruction of three more G3Ms following his first kill. These were Wong's final combat claims.

35

Gladiator I 2806 of the 28th FS/5th FLG (Chinese Air Force), flown by Capt Arthur Chin Shui-Tin, Hankow, China, 3 August 1938

'Art' Chin, with 6.5 kills, was the leading Chinese Gladiator pilot, and he flew this aircraft during the action of 3 August 1938. After rescuing his wingman, he was surrounded by Imperial Japanese Navy A5Ms and heavily hit – armour plate fitted from a wrecked I-15 probably saving him. Cornered and unable to break away, Chin managed to ram one of the A5Ms and bring it down, although 2806 also lost its right wings in the collision. Its pilot then experienced great difficulty in getting out of the gyrating wreck, before parachuting to safety. He later flew the surviving Gladiators in a 'guerrilla' war against the Japanese.

36

J-8A Gladiator 284/F of *Flygflottilj* F 19 (Royal Swedish Air Force), flown by 2Lt F H I Iacobi, Lake Kemi, Finland, 12 January 1940

Deployed as a volunteer squadron in support of the Finns, F 19 enjoyed its first air combat success against the Soviets on 12 January 1940 when, during the unit's first mission, 2nd Lt Ian Iacobi brought down an I-15bis over Märkäjärvi. This proved to be the 24-year-old Swede's only air combat success in the brief Winter War, although several of his compatriots made multiple claims. Gladiator 284, which was fitted with a ski undercarriage, had silver paint over-sprayed on its olive green upper surfaces as disruptive camouflage, as well as Finnish markings. This aircraft also made the next F 19 claim when the top-scoring Swedish pilot, 2Lt Per-Johan Salwen, destroyed another I-15 on 17 January. The Gladiator returned to Sweden with F 19, but was written off in an accident on 5 February 1941.

37

Gladiator II GL-255 of LLv 26 (Finnish Air Force), flown by Sgt Oiva Tuominen, Mensunkangas, Finland, 13 February 1940

The leading Finnish Gladiator ace with 6.5 kills was 'Oippa' Tuominen, who's score eventually reached 44. Having already claimed 3.5 Soviet aircraft whilst flying Gladiator GL-258, on the 13th he had a remarkable day by any yardstick. Flying GL-255, Tuominen downed three SB 2s of the 39.SBAP and shared a fourth with another future ace, Lt Lautomaki. Then, during a later patrol he destroyed an R-5 biplane to make it five kills in a day! Like most Winter War Gladiators, GL-255 is fitted with a ski undercarriage, and wears the standard RAF shadow dispensation colours of light and dark shades of dark green and dark earth, with black and white undersides.

38

Gladiator II GL-269 of 1/LLv 26 (Finnish Air Force), flown by Capt Paavo Berg, Utti, Finland, February 1940

Having been hurriedly shipped from Britain and assembled in Sweden, the Gladiator's first victory in Finnish colours was claimed by 'Pate' Berg whilst he was ferrying GL-269 on 2 February 1940. It was also his first kill, and he went on to make his next three claims whilst flying this aircraft – on the 18th he brought down two DB-3s from 1.MTAP and damaged a third. The following day Berg's patrol saw combat with I-153s from 149.IAP, and he shot a fighter down. However, he was flying a different Gladiator when he 'made ace' on 20 February by bringing down another Soviet SB bomber. Berg was the second, and last, Finnish ace on the type. He was killed in action during the Continuation War.

39

Gladiator I 427 of the Norwegian Army Air Service Fighter Wing, flown by Sgt K F Schye, Fornebu, Norway, 9 April 1940

The tiny Norwegian fighter force at the time of the German invasion consisted of a handful of Gladiators that still wore peacetime markings – silver overall, with striped Norwegian colours on the wings and rudder. The Luftwaffe was engaged by the *Jagevingen* early on 9 April, with several aircraft being shot down, although in the confusion there were some double claims. One undisputed victory was that of Sgt Kristian Schye, who attacked a Bf 110 which force-landed at Voyen, its crew briefly becoming PoWs. Schye was then hit by another Bf 110 and wounded, forcing him to land his damaged fighter. He survived, escaped capture and later became a doctor.

40

Gladiator I G-32 of the *1ére Escadrille de Chasse* ('le Comete'), *1ére Groupe 2me Regiment* (Belgian Army Air Service), flown by 1/Sgt Henri Winand, Beauvechain, Belgium, 11 May 1940

The Gladiators of the Belgian Army saw a limited amount of combat during the first days of the German *blitzkrieg* of May 1940. Retaining their pre-war colours of olive green and aluminium, they were decorated with blue rudders and the *Escadrille's* red comet flash on the fuselage. Most avoided destruction on the ground, but five were shot down by Bf 109s on the first morning of the invasion. The following morning, six of the survivors escorted Battles sent to attack German Panzers, but they were again hit by Bf 109s of JG 1 and most downed in a one-sided fight, although Henri Winand was credited with damaging a fighter. This, and Sgt Rolin's 'probably damaged', were the only Belgian Gladiator claims.

BIBLIOGRAPHY

Attard, Joseph, *The Battle of Malta.* William Kimber, 1980

Ambrose, James, *Gathering of Eagles.* Brown Purnell, 1974

Baker, E C R, *Ace of Aces.* William Kimber, 1965

Bowyer, Chaz and Christopher Shores, *Desert Air Force at War.* Ian Allan, 1981

Bowyer, Michael J F, *Fighting Colours.* PSL, 1969

Brown, Robin A, *Shark Squadron - History of 112 Squadron.* Crecy, 1994

Cull, Brian, with Bruce Lander and Heinrich Weiss, *Twelve Days in May.* Grub St, 1995

Cull, Brian, with Don Minterne, *Hurricanes over Tobruk.* Grub St, 1999

Dahl, Roald, *Going Solo.* Jonathan Cape, 1986

Franks, Norman L R, *RAF Fighter Command.* PSL, 1992

Franks, Norman L R, *Fighter Command Losses Vol 1.* Midland, 1997

Halley, James J, *Squadrons of the RAF & Commonwealth.* Air Britain, 1988

Halley, James J, *The K File (The RAF in the 1930s).* Air Britain, 1995

Halley, James J, *RAF Aircraft L1000-N9999.* Air Britain, 1993

Halliday, Hugh, *'Woody' - A Fighter Pilot's Album.* CANAV Books, 1987

Hunt, Leslie, *Twenty One Squadrons - History of the Royal Auxiliary Air Force.* Garnstone Press, 1972

Jackson, Robert, *The Forgotten Aces.* Sphere Books, 1989

Jefford, C G, Wg Cdr, *RAF Squadrons.* Airlife, 1988

Low, Martin, and Stefaan Bouwer, *South African Air Force at War.* Chris van Rensburg Publications, 1995

Marchant, David, *Rise from the East - History of 247 Sqn.* Air Britain, 1996

Mason, Frank K, *Gloster Gladiator.* Macdonald, 1964

Minterne, Don, *History of 73 Sqn Part 1.* Tutor, 1994

Netherwood, G, *Desert Squadron.* Schindler, 1944

Piper, Ian, *We Never Slept - History of 605 Sqn.* 605 Sqn Association, 1996

Pitchfork, Graham, *Men Behind the Medals.* Pen & Sword, 1998

Popham, Hugh, *Into Wind.* Hamish Hamilton,1969

Rawlings, John D R, *Fighter Squadrons of the RAF.* Macdonald, 1969

Rawlings, John D R, *Pictorial History of the Fleet Air Arm.* Ian Allan, 1973

Richards, Denis, *RAF Official History 1939-45 Vol 1.* HMSO, 1953

Rogers, Anthony, *Battle over Malta.* Sutton, 2000

Shores, Christopher, *Mediterranean Air War Vol 1.* Ian Allan, 1972

Shores, Christopher and Heinz Ring, *Fighters over the Desert.* Neville Spearman, 1969

Shores, Christopher, *Strike True - History of 80 Sqn.* Air Britain, 1986

Shores, Christopher, Brian Cull and Nicola Meliza, *Air War for Yugoslavia, Greece and Crete.* Grub St, 1987

Shores, Christopher, Brian Cull and Nicola Meliza, *Malta - the Hurricane Years.* Grub St, 1987

Shores, Christopher, et al, *Fledgling Eagles.* Grub St, 1991

Shores, Christopher, et al, *Dust Clouds over the Middle East.* Grub St, 1996

Shores, Christopher, and Clive Williams, *Aces High Vol 1.* Grub St, 1994

Shores, Christopher, *Aces High Vol 2.* Grub St, 1999

Sturtivant, Ray, and Theo Ballance, *Squadrons of the Fleet Air Arm.* Air Britain, 1994

Sturtivant, Ray, and Mick Burrow, *Fleet Air Arm Aircraft 1939-1945.* Air Britain, 1995

Wisdom, T H, *Wings over Olympus.* Alton & Unwin, 1942

INDEX

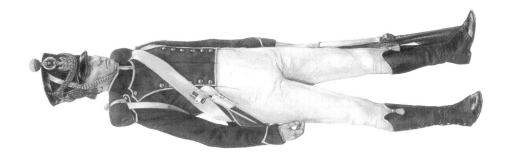

OSPREY PUBLISHING

FIND OUT MORE ABOUT OSPREY

❑ Please send me a FREE trial issue
of Osprey Military Journal

❑ Please send me the latest listing of Osprey's publications

❑ I would like to subscribe to Osprey's e-mail newsletter

Title/rank _____

Name _____

Address _____

_____

_____

Postcode/zip _____ state/country _____

e-mail _____

Which book did this card come from?

_____

❑ I am interested in military history

My preferred period of military history is _____

❑ I am interested in military aviation

My preferred period of military aviation is _____

I am interested in (please tick all that apply)

❑ general history ❑ militaria ❑ model making

❑ wargaming ❑ re-enactment

Please send to:

USA & Canada: Osprey Direct USA, c/o Motorbooks International, P.O. Box 1, 729 Prospect Avenue, Osceola, WI 54020

UK, Europe and rest of world:
Osprey Direct UK, P.O. Box 140, Wellingborough, Northants, NN8 2FA, United Kingdom

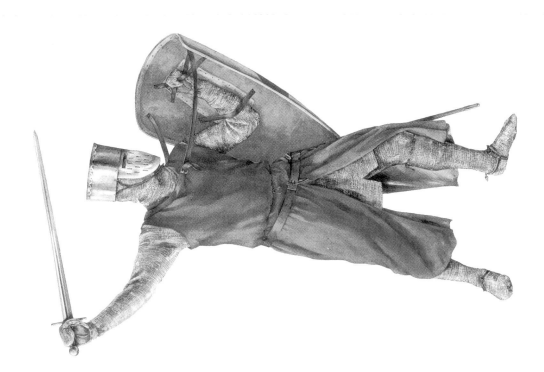

OSPREY
PUBLISHING

www.ospreypublishing.com

call our telephone hotline
for a free information pack

USA & Canada: 1-800-458-0454
UK, Europe and rest of world call:
+44 (0) 1933 443 863

Young Guardsman
Figure taken from *Warrior 22:*
Imperial Guardsman 1799–1815
Published by Osprey
Illustrated by Christa Hook

Knight, c.1190
Figure taken from *Warrior 1: Norman Knight 950 – 1204AD*
Published by Osprey
Illustrated by Christa Hook

POSTCARD